Visual Guide to

Chart Patterns

Since 1996, Bloomberg Press has published books for finance professionals on investing, economics, and policy affecting investors. Titles are written by leading practitioners and authorities, and have been translated into more than 20 languages.

The Bloomberg Financial Series provides both core reference knowledge and actionable information for finance professionals. The books are written by experts familiar with the work flows, challenges, and demands of investment professionals who trade the markets, manage money, and analyze investments in their capacity of growing and protecting wealth, hedging risk, and generating revenue.

Books in the series include:

Visual Guide Candlestick Charting by Michael Thomsett

Visual Guide to Municipal Bonds by Robert Doty

Visual Guide to Financial Markets by David Wilson

Visual Guide to Chart Patterns by Thomas N. Bulkowski

For more information, please visit our Web site at www.wiley.com/go/bloombergpress.

How to Use This Book

The *Visual Guide to ...* series is designed to be a comprehensive and easy-to-follow guide on today's most relevant finance and investing topics. All charts are in full color and presented in a large format to make them easy to read and use. We've also included the following elements to reinforce key information and processes:

- **Definitions:** Terminology and technical concepts that arise in the discussion.
- **Key Points:** Critical ideas and takeaways from the full text.
- **Bloomberg Functionality Cheat Sheet:** For Bloomberg terminal users, a back-of-the-book summary of relevant functions for the topics and tools discussed.

Go Beyond Print

Every Visual Guide is also available as an e-book, which include the following features:

- Video tutorials to show concepts in action.
- Quizzes to reinforce your newfound knowledge and skills.
- Pop-ups with definitions for key terms.

Acknowledgments

I like dealing with the best. That is why writing and publishing a book is made easy by John Wiley & Sons and Pamela van Giessen. Thanks, Pamela.

Thanks also to the other Wiley workers that played their part in acquiring or creating this book: Evan Burton, Meg Freeborn, Chris Gage, and Stephen Isaacs.

Introduction

Sometimes before I trade, an inner voice speaks to me. Some may call it the voice of experience, but I prefer to call it the voice of knowledge and wisdom. When I have listened to that voice, it has saved me money. One goal of this book is to provide the knowledge so that you can create your own trading voice.

Whether you are a professional trader, money manager, or retired schoolteacher trying to boost the inheritance for the grandchildren, this book is for you.

From the expert to the novice, there is information about chart patterns that you do not know or may have forgotten. This book will provide a visual guide to learning about chart patterns in a manner that is simple and easy to understand.

Consider this book an instruction manual for recognizing chart patterns, discovering why they behave as they do, and learning what it means when you see one. You will learn to see not squiggles on price charts, but footprints of the smart money; not a mountain range, but double tops, rectangles, and head-and-shoulders.

The basics come first so that we speak the same language. What you learn in this section may surprise you. The basics provide a foundation for what follows.

Then we cover the most important and popular chart patterns. This is where you discover that not every peak or valley is a chart pattern. What to look for and why they form are in this section.

Completing the book are buy and sell signals. I do not offer mechanical trading systems, but visual ones that can help make you money or avoid losing it.

When you turn the last page of this book, my hope is that you leave with a greater understanding and knowledge of chart patterns, knowledge that can serve as food for the inner trading voice. Should that voice speak to you, listen. It could save you a bundle. And if you find yourself arguing with that inner voice at the grocery store, then blame me.

Visual Guide to

Chart Patterns

THE BASICS

This section of the book reviews the basics: minor highs and lows, trendlines, gaps, throwbacks, pullbacks, support, and resistance. I provide many exhibits so that we agree on terms and techniques. The basics will become important when we move to identifying chart patterns and then using them to signal trades.

that is fine since rarely will peaks or valleys stop at exactly the same price. The line represents a temporary barrier to an upward move.

For the moment, ignore the V-bottom at I. Search below line G for valleys that bottom near the same price. I found them and drew line F. It represents a support area connecting bottoms J and H, and extending to the right with additional touches along the way.

Does the GF trading range mean price is changing trend from down to up? Perhaps. It is too early to tell for sure.

What about the emergency dive to I? That submarine plunge may have been panic selling, forcing the stock down to a level low enough that it represented a steal to value investors. The needle shape of the V bottom supports this theory (that is, price remained at I for just one day before dumping its ballast and rising).

Notice pattern HIJ. It is an inverted (upside down) head-and-shoulders pattern. H and J represent shoulders and I is the head. K could be a cancerous growth on the neck, but lab results have not come back yet. It is not important to the survival of the pattern.

Another head-and-shoulders bottom (a synonym for an inverted head-and-shoulders) occurs at ABC. This one is unusual—and rarer—because price trends upward into the pattern, not downward.

For now, though, the inbound price trend is not important. What is important is to train your eyes to find peaks that top out near the same level and find valleys that bottom near the same price. When you can do that, you can find chart patterns. It is that simple.

Curved Patterns

After finding peaks and valleys that align, try imagining price tracing curves. I show two examples in Exhibit 1.4.

Notice that the price bars at A begin rising, following a straight line of trend, but then curve at the top. Connecting the underside of price bars in a rising price trend often shows the curve better than connecting the tops. Either way is fine.

Pattern A is called an inverted and ascending scallop. The chart pattern appears often on the charts, but it is not popular or well known. The fishy sounding name refers to the bowl shape and not the mollusk. If you find one, never eat it.

The rounding turn at B forms another curved pattern. The B turn would be a rounding bottom, but price needs to enter the pattern trending down and not up. B is an example of a failed cup with handle pattern. The handle is at C. Cups have many qualifications, so strictly speaking, this is not one. However, the pattern does show the important parts: a rising price trend followed by a rounded turn and a short handle.

Diagonal Patterns

Staying with the same chart, look at pattern D on the left. What happened to the rectangle bottom identified in an earlier chart? It is still there, of course, but the new lines form a different chart pattern. Chart patterns can nest (one inside the other) and the same pattern can appear as two different types. Think of it

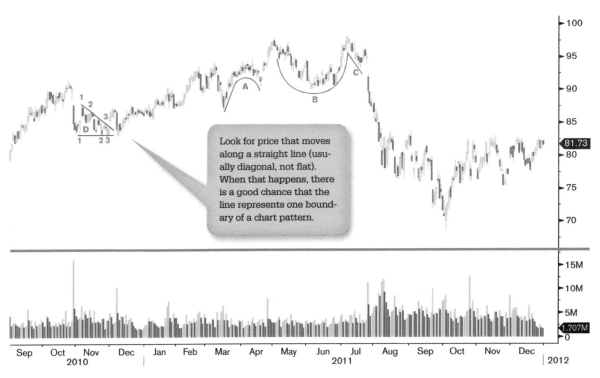

Look for price that moves along a straight line (usually diagonal, not flat). When that happens, there is a good chance that the line represents one boundary of a chart pattern.

Exhibit 1.4: MMM US Equity (3M Co)

as explaining the words "there," "their," and "they're" to someone learning English. They sound the same, but are different.

Look on the chart where price forms diagonals. I show one as a slanting blue trendline above D. The line touches price three times as marked. Another trendline touches the pattern's bottom, also three times. The blue pattern is an example of a descending triangle.

Constructing Patterns

When you look at a price chart, train your eyes to search for peaks that top out near the same price. They may form chart patterns (double tops) that warn of a coming trend change from up to down.

Train your eyes to find valleys that bottom near the same price (double bottoms). Bottoming patterns can

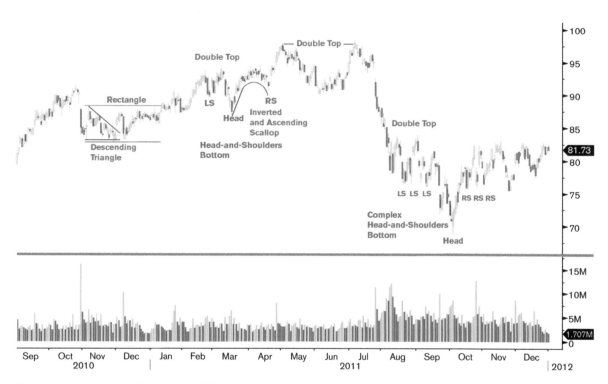

Exhibit 1.5: MMM US Equity (3M Co)

alert you to a stock ready to fly like the model rockets I launched as a kid (not the homemade gasoline one that ignited a water puddle—sorry about that, Mom).

Patterns that form diagonals (descending triangle, for example) or curves (scallops, rounding bottoms, or cup with handles) also foretell the direction that price may take.

Visually connect peaks, valleys, curves, and diagonals to form chart patterns.

Exhibit 1.5 highlights the valid patterns identified so far.

LS means left shoulder and RS means right shoulder. A complex head-and-shoulders bottom (lower right) takes the place of the rectangle bottom.

A complex head-and-shoulders bottom has multiple shoulders and multiple heads, but rarely both.

Think of pattern recognition as like trying to find the Big Dipper or Cassiopeia in the heavens at night.

In the next chapter, I begin to develop a common language, starting with minor highs and lows. Do not be alarmed. This is not as hard as learning French. However, I could be lying because I never learned French.

Test Yourself

Decide which of the following statements are true or false.

1. Overhead resistance occurs when price stalls or reverses, and is always below price.
2. Underlying support happens when price stalls at the same level as it has in the past. Support is never above price.
3. A rectangle forms between underlying resistance and overhead support.
4. On the same price scale (daily scale or weekly scale, but not mixed), tall chart patterns tend to outperform smaller ones.
5. The same price pattern can have multiple names.
6. Like an expectant mother, one price pattern can be inside another.

Answers: 1. False; 2. True; 3. False; 4. True; 5. True; 6. True

CHAPTER 2

Minor Highs and Lows

Minor highs and lows are synonyms for peaks and valleys except that they have strict definitions that can help with pattern recognition. I will use these terms throughout this book, so we might as well go through the pain of learning what they mean and how to recognize them.

A minor high does not refer to an overdose, and a minor low is not lingo for a bad trip. Rather, they represent the building blocks of pattern recognition. If you can program a computer to find them, then you can automate pattern recognition. For example, a triple top has three minor highs near the same price.

Since you are a human computer, I have created definitions for minor highs and lows to help you find them until your eyes become trained to spot them. String them together in your mind and patterns will emerge, patterns that repeat, patterns that can make you money.

Peaks: Minor Highs

A minor high is a significant peak on the price chart. What does *significant* mean? I had to answer that question when I wrote Patternz—free software that automatically finds chart patterns. I discovered that peaks between three and five days apart led to the best pattern recognition (the exact number is pattern specific).

Use five days between peaks for minor highs, but be flexible.

Exhibit 2.1 shows each peak highlighted with an asterisk that is at least five days away from a higher peak. For example, point A is the highest high from at least five days before to five days after the peak.

Notice that peak B does not have an asterisk. According to my computer, it is not a minor high. Why? Because C has a high that is above peak B, and C is five days away from B.

Exhibit 2.1: GE US Equity (General Electric Co)

The same situation occurs at D with a higher high occurring three days later. Nevertheless, I consider peaks B and D to be minor highs. Grasp the concept that a minor high is a significant peak in a price trend and worry less about counting days between peaks. Once you train your eyes to see minor highs, you will not need to count. It also helps if you are sober.

Valleys: Minor Lows

In a manner similar to minor highs, minor lows are valleys separated by at least five days from a lower low. That means five days before to five days after the minor low.

Exhibit 2.2 shows an example, with asterisks highlighting minor lows.

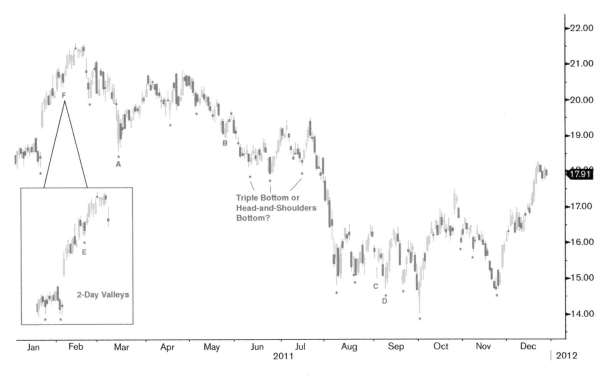

Exhibit 2.2: GE US Equity (General Electric Co)

For example, valley A is below the adjacent price bars such that none are lower than it is for at least five days on either side.

Look at B. Notice the absence of an asterisk. If you count five candles to the right of B, you will see that a price bar is slightly lower than B (it may be hard to tell, so just take my word for it). Candle B is not strictly a minor low, but I consider it one anyway.

Candle C is another example of a bottom that is not strictly a minor low because it is too close to lower candles. However, if this were the left shoulder of a head-and-shoulders bottom, then I would probably consider it a valid minor low.

In other words, be flexible when searching for minor lows. If it looks like price is making a turn, then it is a minor low. If you need to count the price bars to be sure it is a minor low, then do so.

The inset shows bottoms with two days of separation instead of five, highlighted with asterisks. Notice that point E qualifies, but does it look like a minor low? No. It appears as part of the upward price trend and not a significant turning point. It is not a minor low.

In the next chapter, I discuss trendlines, and there are three types. Can you name them?

Need a hint? One is curved, but the others are not straight and diagonal. Wait until you read my exercises. You may find it easier to eat a bowling ball than to get them right!

For Further Reading

You may find my free website useful, including the link to Patternz:

Over 500 articles on chart patterns: www.thepatternsite.com

Free pattern recognition software that finds 66 chart patterns and 105 candlesticks: www.thepatternsite.com/patternz.html

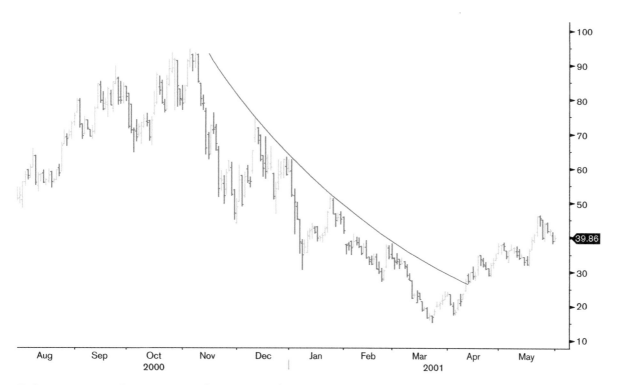

Exhibit 3.2: ABGX US Equity (Abgenix Inc)

valleys with a straight line, highlighting an up-sloping trend.

For example, Exhibit 3.5 shows price trending at blue line A (far left). The line works well, meaning it follows the minor lows until F, G, and H. Those candles poke through the line. In fact, H begins a new trend downward.

Line B shows a horizontal price trend, also drawn along the minor lows. Trendlines C and D are about the same length as A and at nearly the same slope.

As you experiment with drawing trendlines, you may discover that steep, up-sloping trendlines do not last long. Why? Because traders take profits if the stock rises too fast. That selling pressure will force the

Exhibit 3.3: INTC US Equity (Intel Corp)

stock to move sideways or down, piercing the trend-line—at least temporarily.

Shallower trendlines tend to be powerhouses. From them, strong moves are born. In between the shallow and vertical trendlines are the also-rans. They show breaks in the prevailing short- to intermediate-term trend only to see a new trend emerge, perhaps at a shallower angle.

Look at trendline E, drawn in red. It is the longest on the chart, and it is also the most important. Why? Because price plunges through it in July, signaling the end of the uptrend.

Notice that I have drawn each up-sloping trendline along the valleys and not the tops. Why? To signal a trend change. Up-sloping trendlines drawn along peaks will not do that.

Exhibit 3.4: INTC US Equity (Intel Corp)

Trendline Types: Internal, External, and Curved

Trendline A is (Exhibit 3.5) called an internal trend-line because it slices through price at F and G (H does not count because it ends the trend).

The thinking behind drawing internal trendlines is that the line best represents the majority of traders. Few will receive a fill at the day's exact high or low, so why draw a trendline connecting those outliers?

I have a different view. If I were to place a stop be-low the trendline, I do not want to be stopped out be-cause my trendline sliced through price and an outlier hit my stop. I prefer to draw my trendlines like line C. This line follows the price bottoms as it trends. Line C is an example of an external trendline. An external trendline connects only the price ends; it does not slice through price.

Line I represents the third type of trendline: a curved trendline. It begins straight, but curves over

DEFINITION:
Internal trendline

An internal trendline slices through price.

DEFINITION:
External trendline

An external trendline hugs the end of price.

DEFINITION:
Curved trendline

A curved trendline also hugs price, but it is curved (although a curved trendline can be external or internal, too).

Steep trendlines stop trending sooner than shallow ones.

Exhibit 3.5: MMM US Equity (3M Co)

KEY POINT:

Draw trendlines for the best fit, whether they look curved or slice through price.

at the top of the inverted and ascending scallop chart pattern. Curved trendlines become important for some chart patterns and for parabolic moves (curved moves that resemble a biplane flying level then going vertical).

Draw trendlines for the best fit. If a trendline happens to slice through price, do not get your knickers in a twist. If a curved line better represents a trend, then use it.

Downtrend Connections

Down trendlines are the same as up trendlines except you draw them along peaks. Why? To detect a trend change.

Exhibit 3.6 shows an example of several trendlines highlighting a falling stock. Line A is short and steep. It is an external trendline that touches the candle tops three times.

I originally drew line B from the start in May until point B, but then extended it. It touched another candle at the line's end, forming a chart pattern called a bump and run reversal bottom. The pattern predicts an upward breakout, which is what happened. I used to call them bump and run formations but changed it because of the acronym (BARF).

Line C, drawn in red, is a major trendline not only for its length, but also because it signals a trend change. Price not only slices through the line at E, but closes above it. A new up trend may be underway.

Minor low D finds support near the trendline, too, although price pierced the trendline for a day before reversing. The E to D move is a throwback, a pattern I will discuss in a later chapter.

Notice the two chart patterns outlined in blue on the far left of the chart. Those are broadening tops. A top trendline connects the peaks and a bottom trendline connects the valleys, creating a megaphone appearance.

If you know how to draw trendlines, you probably could have found these two patterns. Not only do trendlines signal a trend change, but they also outline pattern boundaries.

On a price chart, look for peaks that align. Draw trendlines connecting them to see what they reveal. Draw trendlines along valleys and see what they show,

too. This is especially significant along the hard right edge (the right side of the chart) because trends there suggest where price is going in the future.

The two videos describe a methodology for drawing trendlines and how to detect a trend change.

Video:
Detecting Trend Changes in Down Trends

www.wiley.com/go/bulkowskivg/Video1

Video:
Detecting Trend Changes in Up Trends

www.wiley.com/go/bulkowskivg/Video2

Trendline Guidelines

Now that we have experimented with drawing trendlines, what are the guidelines and tips for their use? Here is a nine-item list.

1. Trendlines should connect at least two peaks (minor highs) or two valleys (minor lows), preferably three or more.
2. Like horseshoes and hand grenades, closeness counts. Price need not touch the trendline, but it should come close.
3. To detect a trend change, draw trendlines along the valleys when price is trending up. Draw trendlines along the peaks in a declining stock.

DEFINITION:
Trendlines

Trendlines not only follow trends, but also outline chart patterns.

Exhibit 3.6: ACET US Equity (Aceto Corp)

4. Trendlines with widely spaced touches are more significant than are those with narrow ones (I proved this).

5. In 2006, I wrote in my book *Getting Started in Chart Patterns*, "Trendlines are like diving boards. You get a bigger bounce from a longer diving board than a shorter one."

6. Steep trendlines underperform shallow ones. That means larger moves occur after a trendline pierce from a shallow trendline than a steep one.

7. Rising volume along an up-sloping trendline *powers* (a larger decline) price downward after a trendline break more than does a receding volume trend leading to the breakout.

8. For downward sloping trendlines, receding volume leads to better performance after price pierces the trendline, moving up.

9. Just because price closes above a down-sloping trendline or below an up-sloping one is no reason to believe that the trend has changed. It is only a hint of a trend change, not a guarantee.

The next chapter discusses one of the most important topics: support and resistance. If you can determine when price is going to reverse, you can make a bundle. If you save wisely and invest carefully, you can retire at 36 just as I did. Learning about support and resistance is a good first step to achieving that goal.

This just in: All you have to do is turn the page!

For Further Reading

Bulkowski, Thomas N. *Getting Started in Chart Patterns.* Hoboken, NJ: John Wiley & Sons, 2006.

Bulkowski, Thomas N. *Trading Classic Chart Patterns.* Hoboken, NJ: John Wiley & Sons, 2002.

Test Yourself

Decide which of the following statements are true or false.

1. To detect a trend change in a rising price trend, draw trendlines along the peaks.
2. To detect a trend change in a falling price trend, draw trendlines along the valleys.
3. When price closes above a down-sloping trendline or below an up-sloping one, it hints of a coming trend change.
4. An internal trendline cuts through price.
5. You should avoid using internal trendlines.
6. A straight trendline on the logarithmic scale will appear curved on the linear scale.
7. When trying to measure physical distances, use the linear scale.

Answers: 1. False; 2. False; 3. True; 4. True; 5. False; 6. True; 7. True

CHAPTER 4

Support and Resistance

If trendlines are like hammers, then support and resistance (SAR) are like boards. Price stalls or even reverses at SAR areas and that makes predicting future price trends easier. Fortunately, there are many techniques that show SAR, and this chapter discusses them.

In the fall of 1987, a friend of mine said that she had purchased shares in a mutual fund. This was her first time investing in the stock market, and she was excited!

On black Monday, October 19, 1987, the Dow Jones industrials lost over 22 percent of their value in *one* session.

She was not excited! In fact, she vowed to sell as soon as she got her money back, which she did.

Her behavior is typical of novices. Imagine that others acted the same way. Their emotional selling would force price down. People buying the stock just before the drop or as the selling begins also get upset as the stock tumbles. They vow to sell when they get their money back, too.

If you were to plot this behavior on a chart, you would see the stock peak and then peak again near the same price. That concerted selling forms a barrier to upward movement called overhead resistance. Price will eat through that resistance, so it is not made of concrete.

A similar behavior pattern exists for valleys. People want to buy a stock at $10, but price gaps higher and zooms away from them, rising to $15. They missed the move and vow to buy the stock if it ever gets back to $10.

When the stock drops to $10, they buy, joining others doing the same thing. That buying demand builds a floor underneath the stock, which we call support. The floor is not made of concrete either, so price can act as termites do and eat its way through.

Support and resistance is human nature at work—a pictorial representation of emotion.

DEFINITION:
Overhead resistance
Overhead resistance occurs when selling pressure overcomes buying demand, sending price lower—at least for a time.

DEFINITION:
Support
Underlying support occurs when buying demand overcomes selling pressure, putting a temporary floor beneath the stock.

Exhibit 4.1: ANF US Equity (Abercrombie & Fitch Co)

Support and resistance represent *areas* or *bands* where price is likely (but not guaranteed) to stall or reverse. Price can motor through a support zone and a week later, it will stop there as if taking a snooze at a roadside rest stop.

Trendline SAR

Trendlines highlight and act as SAR areas. For example, Exhibit 4.1 shows a trendline connecting the valleys beginning at A, touching B, C, D, and E. At F, however, price pierces the trendline, heading down.

Notice that at G, H, and I, price bumps up against a ceiling formed by the same trendline. The trendline that once acted as support now acts as resistance.

The blue trendline shows the same principle, but not as clearly. The trendline acts as support from J to M and as overhead resistance at N and O.

After drawing a trendline, imagine what price might do in the future. By extending trendline AF,

> **KEY POINT:**
> Support areas can act as resistance and resistance areas can act as support.

Price closes an exhaustion gap (H) 64 percent of the time within a week, on average, in a bull market.

Exhibit 4.5: AWI US Equity (Armstrong World Industries Inc)

will use 20 as a sell point, and if enough actually sell, price will reverse there. Beat the crowds and sell at 19.95.

Day traders can use round numbers, too, as targets. When price reaches a round number, consider selling.

SAR at Peaks, Valleys, and Chart Patterns

Support and resistance forms at peaks, valleys, and chart patterns. Exhibit 4.5 shows examples of all three.

Starting on the left, an ascending triangle appears at G. The horizontal consolidation region has a flat top, but it looks loose with price wandering up and down between the two red trendlines. That region should show support or resistance in the future, and it does. The symmetrical triangle forms in the middle of the HCR and point I on the far right also peaks near the top of G.

H is an exhaustion gap. Notice that price later finds support at the bottom of the gap.

The symmetrical triangle is a delight because it is a perfect example of the chart pattern. Price bounces from trendline to trendline, filling the pattern with movement. The tops and bottoms of the pattern touch each trendline without leaving whiskers behind for your shaver.

Notice that price turns at A, directly above the triangle apex. I will discuss this behavior in a later chapter (see Chapter 26).

The apex is also a place of future support and resistance (as is the entire triangle, for that matter). Although valley B slides below the apex, it does reverse within the triangle.

The horizontal red line joining peaks C and D show peak SAR. Price bumps up against a ceiling there. During an advance, expect price to reverse at the level of a prior peak (it may not, so keep that in mind, too).

This idea also applies to valleys. Circled in blue is a loose horizontal congestion region at E. When price attempts to exceed this level at F, it hits the HCR and finds overhead resistance.

Finally, price drops to find support at K setup by peak J (and the loose congestion area to its left).

When looking at price trends, imagine where price may stall or reverse. Those reversals can happen at the price level of prior peaks, prior valleys, horizontal congestion regions, gaps, trendlines, chart patterns, and round numbers.

It sounds like I am covering every possible number on the price chart, right? Have faith that price will reverse at support or resistance and when it fails, squeal like a stuck pig.

The next chapter discusses four types of gaps. Traders love gaps. Why? I have no idea. I prefer women.

Test Yourself

Answer the following to test your knowledge of support and resistance.

1. Which of the following do not usually show support or resistance?
   A. Trendlines
   B. Gaps
   C. Chart Patterns
   D. Horizontal consolidation regions
   E. Peaks
   F. Valleys
   G. Whole numbers
   H. The kitchen sink

2. True or false: Support is always beneath price.

3. If price peaks at $10, at what price can you expect resistance in the future?
   A. $10
   B. $10.50
   C. $9.50
   D. None of the above.
   E. All of the above, including D.

4. True or false: To help avoid stop running, never place a stop loss order at a round number.

5. What is meant by support?
   A. Price rises only to bump up against a ceiling and stop rising.
   B. Price drops and then bounces upward as if it has found a floor.
   C. A stock moves in a manner similar to other stocks in the same industry.
   D. Price peaks at $10 and a month later, it forms a minor high at $9.50.

6. True or false: Support areas can also act as resistance areas.

Answers: 1. G and H; 2. True; 3. E; 4. True; 5. B; 6. True

CHAPTER 5

Gaps

There are several types of gaps, but we will cover only four of them. Others, like the ex-dividend gap and the opening gap, are inconsequential or too advanced.

Gaps are exciting! Those that appear at a chart pattern breakout can push a stock like a booster stage does to a rocket. For example, breakout day gaps in symmetrical triangles (bull markets, up breakouts) show gains averaging 36 percent compared to 28 percent for those without gaps.

Sometimes the booster stage fails to ignite as it does in ascending triangles. There, gaps hurt performance: 29 percent versus 35 percent gain for those with and without gaps, respectively.

Being able to tell the gap type can help traders decipher what will happen with the stock. Will a stock begin a new price trend as it does after a breakaway gap, or will an exhaustion gap signal the party is over faster than champagne left uncorked?

Four Types

I show a bar chart to find examples of the four major gap types: area, breakaway, continuation, and exhaustion. The bar chart makes finding gaps easier. (See Exhibit 5.1.)

Look at gap B1, located to the right of the circled congestion region. A breakaway gap always leaves a congestion area. A congestion area is where price moves sideways for a time. It can be just a few days wide—or more—like that circled. The breakaway gap breaks away from the area, hence its name.

Slaloming downhill, we find gap E1. This is an example of an exhaustion gap. The gap exhausts the trend, thus its name. After an exhaustion gap, expect to see a quick reversal, sometimes a powerful one, but also one that does not last long.

Gap A1, on the far left of the chart, is an area gap. These little stinkers carry a load in their pants. They look like breakaway gaps, but a trend does not develop. The gap closes quickly by curling around and filling the gap.

DEFINITION:
Gap closes

A gap is said to close when future price action covers the same price level as the gap. Price fills the gap, closing it.

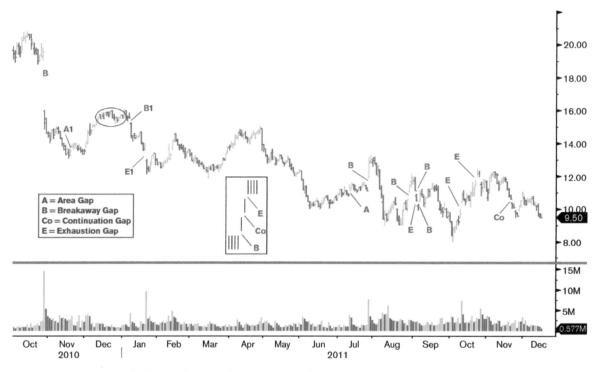

Exhibit 5.1: JNY US Equity (Jones Group Inc/The)

The inset shows an ideal example of the last type of gap, a continuation gap. A trend develops with a breakaway gap (B) that appears after a congestion region. Then a continuation gap appears (Co) during the trend. An exhaustion gap (E) ends the trend.

A continuation gap is also known as a measuring gap because it sometimes forms midway in a price trend. Continuation gaps are rare, and I found only one on the far right of the chart.

Identification Guidelines

What differentiates gaps? The following table describes what to look for.

Gap Type	Discussion
Area, Common, or Pattern:	Occurs in areas of congestion (trendless markets) and close rapidly. Volume on the day of the gap can be high, but returns to normal in a day or two. No significant highs (in uptrends) or lows (in downtrends) occur immediately after the gap. A distinctive curl as the gap closes is a key indication of this gap type.
Breakaway:	Identifies the start of a new trend and occurs on breakout from a consolidation region. Is accompanied by high volume on the day of the gap and continuing for several days. The trend continues long enough for several new highs (for uptrends) or new lows (downtrends) to occur after the gap.
Continuation, Measuring, or Runaway:	Happens in the midst of a straight-line advance or decline. Price continues making new highs or lows without filling the gap. Volume is usually high, propelling price in the direction of the trend.
Exhaustion:	Occurs at the end of a trend on high volume. The gap is not followed by new minor highs or minor lows and the gap itself may be unusually tall. After the gap, price consolidates. Commonly occurs after a continuation gap. The gap closes quickly, usually within a week.

I studied each gap type and found that area gaps close in an average of 3 days.

Breakaway gaps take an average of 136 days to close in a bull market, upward trend, and 168 days in a downward trend.

Continuation gaps close in an average of 98 days (uptrends) and 77 days (downtrends).

Exhaustion gaps close in 9 days (uptrends) and 14 days (downtrends).

Exercise

When I visit my dentist every year, I pull out the *Highlights* magazine and search the drawing for a comb, rake, toothbrush, and other utensils hidden on the page. The exercises that accompany several chapters in this book are just like that search except that here you are looking for chart patterns.

The next chart tests your knowledge of gaps, based on the earlier table and discussion. Try to identify each gap. The numbers point to the gaps and the associated volume. All four gap types appear in Exhibit 5.2.

Exhibit 5.3 shows the answers.

Breakaway gaps exit a congestion area as if it were on fire, so they are easy to spot. Sometimes, however, they become area gaps. Continuation gaps are rare and will appear only in strong price trends. It took a while to find a chart that had them. Exhaustion gaps end a trend, so look for a strong trend, and find a gap that leads to a consolidation region.

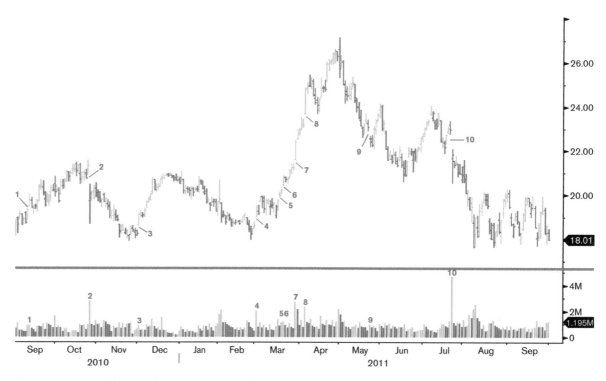

Exhibit 5.2: OLN US Equity (Olin Corp)

Trading Gaps

If you are a day trader, the only gaps important to you are opening gaps. Other intraday gaps that may appear happen because of low volume. Ignore them.

If you are a swing trader, then gaps are important. When a gap forms out of a consolidation region on high volume, you know that a trend is underway. It is a buy signal (but not one you should necessarily take).

If a trend fails to appear, then the gap becomes an area gap. That situation should become clear if the gap closes in two or three price bars. If the gap closes, exit the trade immediately.

Area gaps show a hook as price curls back to the gap. That hook should happen within a handful of price bars of the gap. If it does not, then it is a breakaway gap.

Exhibit 5.3: OLN US Equity (Olin Corp)

When a gap appears in a strong price trend that is already underway, it is probably an exhaustion gap. It could be a continuation gap, so waiting another price bar or two should provide confirmation, and perhaps a better exit price. If you see lots of overlap between one gap bar and the next, then it is an exhaustion gap and time to sell. If the trend continues with little overlap, then it is a continuation gap.

Since continuation gaps are rare, a gap in a trend already underway is most likely an exhaustion gap.

Gap Measure Rule

For continuation gaps, measure from the start of the trend to the middle of the gap and project upward from the middle of the gap to get a price target.

For example, in Exhibit 5.3, continuation gap 7 shows a trend start at A that ends at B. The gap is about midway in the trend. To put numbers to this, the low at A is at 18.95 and the middle of the gap is at 21.57 for a height of 2.62. That gives a target of 21.57 + 2.62 or 24.19. The high at B is at 25.45

Some say that continuation gaps follow breakaway gaps (I have not verified this). If the trend is already underway, but a breakaway gap did not appear, then you are probably looking at an exhaustion gap. Also, exhaustion gaps can be very large. If the gap you are seeing is tall, then it is probably an exhaustion gap.

If you do see an exhaustion gap, consider trading the new direction. Violent reversals can accompany an exhaustion gap. Gaps 8 and 9 in Exhibit 5.3 are examples. Notice that the new trend lasts for about a week, so you have to be nimble trading these.

Now that we have filled the *gaps* in your knowledge, what comes next? Throwbacks and pullbacks. Do you know the difference between them, besides spelling? Hint: Chart patterns that have throwbacks often perform worse than patterns missing them. What about pullbacks? Are pullbacks to stocks what fullbacks are to football? I have no idea what that means.

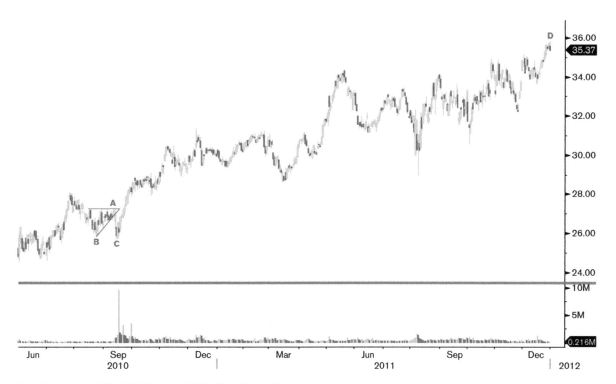

Exhibit 6.2: UIL US Equity (UIL Holdings Corp)

Characteristic	Discussion
Chart pattern breakout	From a chart pattern, price breaks out upward in a throwback and downward in a pullback.
Loop	Price continues in the direction of the breakout for a few days, but then loops back to the breakout price.
White space	After the stock returns to the breakout price, it leaves white space on the chart between the breakout and return.
Time	The stock must return to the breakout price or trendline boundary within 30 days.

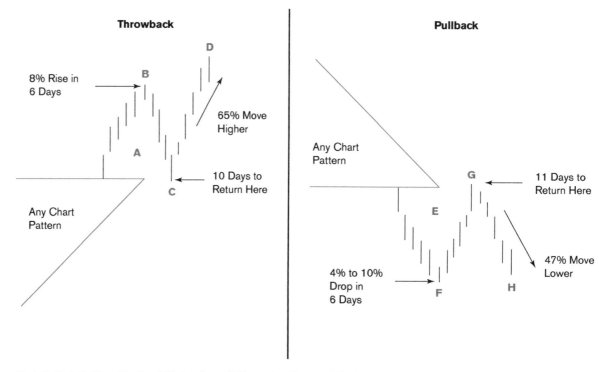

Throwback

8% Rise in 6 Days →

B

D

65% Move Higher

A

10 Days to Return Here ←

C

Any Chart Pattern

Pullback

Any Chart Pattern

G

11 Days to Return Here ←

E

47% Move Lower

4% to 10% Drop in 6 Days →

F

H

Exhibit 6.3 The Typical Behavior of Throwbacks and Pullbacks

Look at Exhibit 6.3, which helps explain the *average* behavior of throwbacks and pullbacks.

The left panel shows a throwback. Buying enthusiasm pushes price upward until it explodes out the top of any chart pattern. However, that buying demand slowly fades in the face of mounting selling pressure. In an average of six days, the stock has peaked after climbing 8 percent. Then it begins the return trip to the chart pattern.

The return takes only four days to either touch or come near the trendline boundary or breakout price, for a total of 10 days to make the round trip.

From there, price may continue lower or it may rebound immediately. In 65 percent of the cases, price resumes the upward breakout direction and rises. The other 35 percent close below the bottom of the chart pattern.

Pullbacks show a similar pattern except they apply to downward breakouts from any chart pattern. Price shoots lower at the breakout when excessive selling overpowers weak buying demand.

In an average of six days, the stock has bottomed and buying demand reverses the downtrend. The return journey takes five days for a total of eleven for the round trip from breakout to pullback.

Price may continue rising from there, and in 53 percent of the cases it does by closing above the top of the chart pattern. The remaining 47 percent of the time, the stock drops.

Exhibit 6.3 shows averages of thousands of chart patterns, so each individual case may vary.

Not all chart patterns will throwback or pullback, either. The accompanying table shows the throwback and pullback rates for popular chart patterns.

The highest throwback rate is for rectangle tops, and triple tops have the highest pullback rate. Descending triangles have the lowest throwback rate and rectangle tops have the lowest pullback rate.

This chapter ends the boot camp. The next chapter begins playing with live ammo by discussing individual chart patterns. It is an exciting time, so gather the children, and you may want to make popcorn.

Chart Pattern	Throwback Rate	Pullback Rate
Ascending triangles	60%	56%
Descending triangles	50%	55%
Double bottoms	56%	N/A
Double tops	N/A	57%
Head-and-shoulders bottoms	57%	N/A
Head-and-shoulders tops	N/A	59%
Rectangle bottoms	59%	59%
Rectangle tops	64%	54%
Symmetrical triangles	58%	58%
Triple bottoms	58%	N/A
Triple tops	N/A	63%
N/A: Not applicable		

Test Yourself

Answer the following questions.

1. True or false: A pullback occurs when price pulls back to the chart pattern from above.

2. True or false: A throwback never happens after a downward breakout.

3. If price breaks out downward from a descending triangle at $10 and 31 days later it is at $10, what has happened?
   A. A throwback has occurred.
   B. A pullback has occurred.
   C. Nothing.

4. Price completes a pullback after a breakout. What is the probability that price will continue higher?
   A. Over 50 percent.
   B. Under 50 percent.
   C. 50 percent.
   D. Unknown.

Answers: 1. False; 2. True; 3. C; 4. A

PART II

PATTERN IDENTIFICATION

This section focuses on identifying individual chart patterns. How do you find them? What should you look for, and why do they form? I answer these questions and others, as well as ask you to find patterns in the exercises in each chapter.

CHAPTER 7

Rectangles

Now that we are experts at identifying minor highs and lows, drawing trendlines, and knowing what support and resistance look like, let us begin by finding our first chart pattern: a rectangle.

Think of a rectangle as a sewer pipe snaking through a construction site. It has a flat top and flat bottom, and price is a rattlesnake winding its way through the pipe. Exhibit 7.1 shows an example of a rectangle bottom.

After trending downward, the stock bumped up against an invisible ceiling of overhead resistance and stood on a floor of underlying support from October to December, forming a rectangle bottom.

That ceiling and floor I show as two horizontal trendlines in red. Notice that price touches each trendline three times on the top (1–3) and three on the bottom (4–6). Also notice that price enters the pattern from the top, trending down.

The exit from the chart pattern, called a breakout, is downward in this example, but can be in any direction for rectangles. I highlight the breakout location in the exhibit. Price must *close* below the bottom of the rectangle to stage a downward breakout.

Notice the volume trend. Just before the breakout, volume recedes to a low level. Many times volume will fall off dramatically a day or two before the breakout of most chart patterns (not just rectangles).

Identification Guidelines

Rectangles are rare, so finding them is about as common as seeing a hummingbird in the middle of a housing subdivision. The following table lists the identification guidelines.

Characteristic	Discussion
Price Trend	The short-term price trend leading to the rectangle is downward for bottoms and upward for tops.
Horizontal Trendlines	Two horizontal, or nearly so, trendlines bound price along the top and bottom of the rectangle.

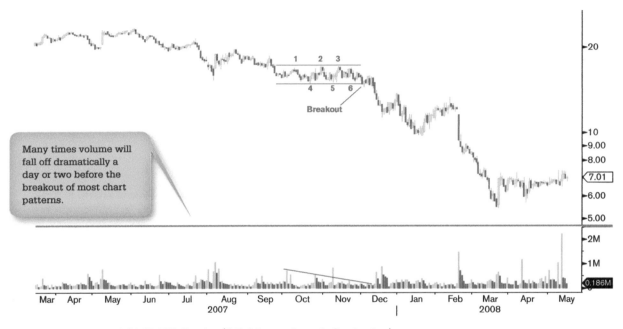

Exhibit 7.1: ACMR US Equity (AC Moore Arts & Crafts Inc)

Characteristic	Discussion
Touches	There should be at least two touches of each trendline.
Volume	For rectangle bottoms: Volume tends to follow the breakout direction: upward for upward breakouts, and downward for downward breakouts. For rectangle tops: Volume usually recedes until the breakout.

When searching a chart for rectangles, begin looking for a congestion region where price moves horizontally, often for weeks. In fact, the average length of 1,228 rectangles in a study I did using daily price data from 1991 to 2011 was 71 days (about 2 1/2 months).

Price should bounce between a support zone at the bottom and resistance at the top.

Connect the minor highs with a horizontal or nearly horizontal trendline. A similar line drawn below the minor lows forms a parallel trendline. Occasionally, one of the trendlines will not be horizontal. That is fine providing the slope is not too steep to disturb the overall picture. Consider the varying trend lengths.

At least two touches (but three is better) of each trendline are required for a valid rectangle. The touches need not alternate from top to bottom, but should have at least two clearly defined minor highs and two minor lows coming close to or touching each trendline.

In the ideal case, the trendline touches should be spaced evenly along the pattern, not bunched together on one end only. In other words, the trendline should not appear like a diving board, with one end unsupported.

To determine whether the rectangle is a top or bottom, look at the price trend leading to the start of the rectangle. Rectangle bottoms have price trending downward into them, but tops have price trending upward. Ignore any overshoot or undershoot in the price bars within a week or so before the start of the rectangle.

For rectangle bottoms, the volume pattern tends to track the breakout direction. For tops, volume often recedes over the length of the rectangle. Do not discard a rectangle because the volume pattern is wrong.

For example, Exhibit 7.2 shows a rectangle top on the weekly scale. Price bounces between two horizontal trendlines B and C, touching each plenty of times, spread along its length. No diving board here!

Price begins the uptrend at A and although price bobbles up and down in early 2004 (before the start of the rectangle), it is clear that this rectangle is at the top of the trend and not at the bottom.

Volume trends upward during the first half of the rectangle and recedes thereafter.

A smaller rectangle appears at E. The price trend off the chart to the left shows that this is a rectangle bottom because price trends downward into it.

Exhibit 7.3 shows a rectangle bottom on the weekly scale. Price trends higher at B, peaks at A, and drops into the rectangle bottom. There, price slides between two horizontal trendlines before breaking out upward.

Notice that the exit trend, C, nearly matches the slope of trendline B. In fact, the exit velocity of price leading out of a chart pattern nearly matches the velocity going into a pattern. That behavior applies not only to rectangles, but to all chart pattern varieties. If you have limited dollars to spend and find two stocks showing chart patterns, choose the one with a higher velocity (cents per day).

Notice that volume, D, slopes upward. This upward slope grows dramatically as price climbs, forming a long hill at E that would scare bicyclists like me trying to climb it.

I also show price undershoot (F) a few weeks before the rectangle begins. Ignore it. Undershoot or overshoot is a short dip or rise, respectively, before the start of a chart pattern. The only influence they have is to confuse novices and give authors like me something to write about.

The inbound price trend is downward leading to this rectangle bottom (starting from A), not upward starting from the undershoot (F).

DEFINITION:
Trend lengths

A short-term trend lasts up to three months. An intermediate-term or secondary trend lasts between three and six months. A long-term trend or primary trend lasts longer than six months.

SMART INVESTOR TIP

Tops have price trending into a chart pattern from the bottom, and bottoms have price trending into a chart pattern from the top.

SMART INVESTOR TIP

The price velocity leading to and exiting from a chart pattern are often similar even if the direction is reversed.

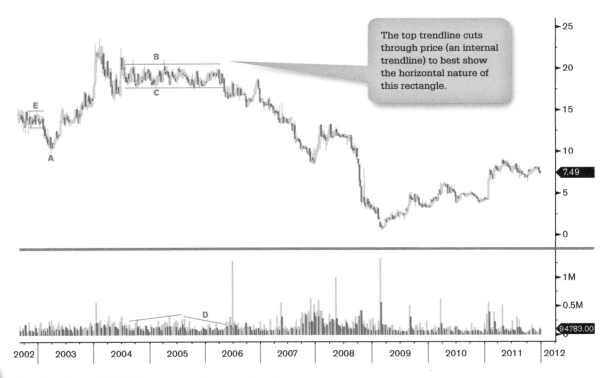

The top trendline cuts through price (an internal trendline) to best show the horizontal nature of this rectangle.

Exhibit 7.2: BSET US Equity (Bassett Furniture Industries Inc)

Rectangle Psychology

Why do rectangles form? Imagine that you run a small mutual fund and your fundamental and technical analysis says that Friedman Industries is a steal at 5.50. You order the trading department to buy the stock at that price. (See Exhibit 7.4.)

Since you want to own several hundred thousand shares and the stock averages only 16,000 shares traded daily, it could take weeks to buy all that you want. Why? Because if you hit the market with an order for 450,000 shares, it will likely send price soaring. That would boost the average cost of ownership.

One tip I learned is that your buying or selling should not be for more than 1 percent of the

One glance at the chart told me all I needed to know, but I checked the news anyway. At A, the company received an offer to merge their operations with another company. These types of buyout offers make the stock soar and then flatline like a dead animal until the merger completes.

I do not consider the pattern to the right of A to be a rectangle. Why? Because of the news surrounding the stock. This is an example of an event pattern—how a stock behaves after it receives a buyout offer.

Exercise

This section presents two exercises. Find the rectangles on each chart. It will help if you look for minor highs that peak near the same price. In your mind, connect those peaks with a horizontal trendline. Then look below that line for minor lows that bottom near the same price. If you find that combination, then you have a rectangle.

Is it a rectangle top or bottom? Look at the short-term price *trend* leading to the rectangle. Tops have price trending upward into the chart pattern and bottoms have price trending downward.

Exhibit 7.7 has at least two rectangles. Find them.

Exhibit 7.8 shows the answer. The pattern highlighted in red is a rectangle bottom. Price begins sliding after A, trending down into the chart pattern, just as it is supposed to do for a rectangle bottom. Then it begins moving horizontally, forming minor highs (1 through 5) and minor lows (6 through 11).

The peak at 1 slices through the top trendline, but does it matter? No. Why not? Because by the time you

recognize the price pattern as a rectangle bottom, that peak ceases to have any significance. Drawing the top trendline above peak 1 would make the other top touches seem too far away.

The same argument applies to valley 8. Price pokes below the red trendline but is not important to the overall picture.

The volume trend (F) rises and price breaks out upward.

Pattern CED is a rectangle top because price trends upward into the chart pattern. Price touches the bottom trendline three times and several times along the top. I drew the top trendline through E to show how price touches the top trendline better. Also, the first bottom touch, B, is part of a straight-line run. It is a minor low, but one that is not easy to see without a trendline connecting it. This is not a perfect example of a rectangle top, but be flexible.

The volume trend (G) is upward even though this rectangle breaks out downward. Rectangle tops often have a receding volume trend, but do not let that throw you off.

Look at pattern J. Did you find this one? The bottom trendline touches only one point. I show it redrawn in the inset as a V-shaped price trend. This V-shape more accurately represents the trend, not a horizontal line.

The top trendline rests on one peak, H. Point I is not a minor high. It is just a price bar on the side of a hill, not an individual peak (minor high). Avoid counting a trendline touch that is not a minor high or minor low. Pattern J is just squiggles on a chart and not a rectangle.

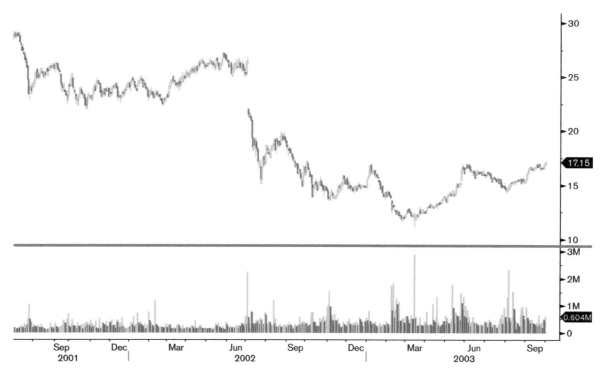

Exhibit 7.7: DPL US Equity (DPL Inc)

Exhibit 7.9 also shows at least one rectangle. Find as many as you can, and have tissues ready in case you get it wrong.

Exhibit 7.10 shows the answers. Let us begin with the red one (C) on the far right, since that is the only rectangle bottom on this chart.

Price trends downward into the chart pattern and then bounces up and down between two horizontal trendlines, touching each at least twice.

Look at peak B. This is an example of overshoot that I mentioned earlier. Price trends upward into the chart pattern, but overshoots the entry for a week

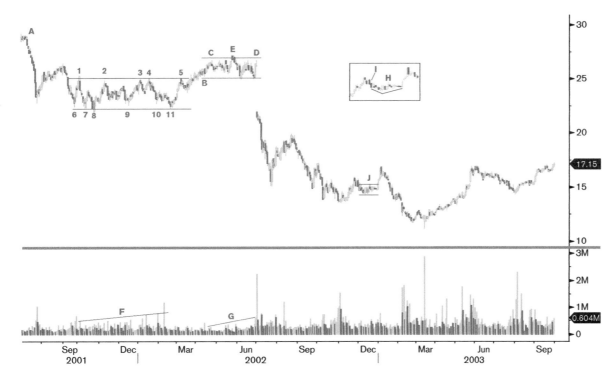

Exhibit 7.8: DPL US Equity (DPL Inc)

or so before sliding into the rectangle. This is a rectangle top.

For rectangle top E, the price trend is horizontal leading to this pattern but upward before that (sharing the same inbound trend as rectangle D). Notice that point A is NOT a minor high so it does not qualify as a top trendline touch. Be careful about touch counts and include only minor highs or minor lows.

Pattern E is a rectangle top. However, I prefer to call pattern DE one long rectangle top instead of thinking of it as two separate ones.

The next chapter discusses ascending triangles. I used to love trading them until I discovered that they did not perform well. In other words, I lost my shirt. Have you seen it?

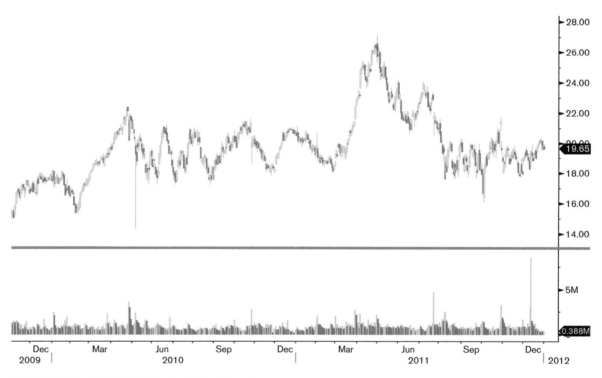

Exhibit 7.9: OLN US Equity (Olin Corp)

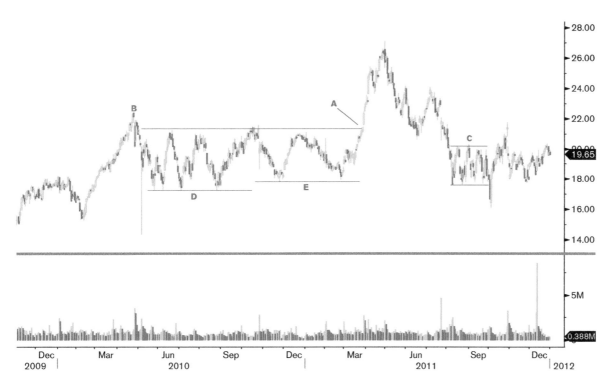

Exhibit 7.10: OLN US Equity (Olin Corp)

Test Yourself

Answer the following statements or questions.

1. True or false: A rectangle bottom *always* has price trending down into the chart pattern.

2. True or false: It is fine if *one* of the trendlines bounding the rectangle bottom is almost horizontal.

3. True or false: It is fine if *both* trendlines are not horizontal, providing they are not too far from level.

4. True or false: A down-sloping volume trend is a key factor in determining whether the chart pattern is a rectangle bottom.

5. True or false: A breakout occurs when price pierces one of the horizontal trendlines.

6. How is a rectangle bottom different from a top (pick all that apply)?

    A. Rectangle bottoms are shorter in duration.

    B. Rectangle bottoms have price entering the chart pattern from the bottom, and tops have it entering from the top, hence the bottom and top names.

    C. They have different names because the volume pattern is different.

    D. A rectangle bottom is a horizontal consolidation region but a top is not.

    E. By definition, price enters tops from the bottom and enters bottoms from the top.

7. True or false: A rectangle top is a horizontal congestion region.

Answers: 1. True; 2. True; 3. True; 4. False; 5. False; 6. E; 7. True

CHAPTER 8

Ascending Triangles

This chapter begins looking at chart patterns not bounded by twin horizontal lines. Triangles use a more complicated shape: diagonal trendlines. Training your eye to recognize them is still easy, though, because the technique builds on what we have learned.

Exhibit 8.1 shows an example of an ascending triangle, highlighted by red trendlines.

Price overshoots (A) the entry to this chart pattern, but who cares? There are no ascending triangle top and bottom variations to worry about (where the inbound price trend is important); there are only ascending triangles.

The stock breaks out upward at B, which happens the majority of the time, but this one sees price quickly turn down, closing below the bottom of the chart pattern at C. When that happens, it busts the ascending triangle.

The popularity of ascending triangles stems from the belief that price will start a robust uptrend.

However, I stopped trading most of them because too many looked like this chart. Price climbed a few percent and then died, killing my trade as well.

Some volume disciples will look at the chart and say, "Look at volume! It should be well above average, but it isn't!" Point D shows the breakout day's volume, and they are right. Volume was well below average, but I have seen profitable trends start on mediocre volume, too. In fact, I do not even show volume on my charts. It is as useful to me as asking if fish like seafood. I am a vegetarian: I eat weeds.

Identification Guidelines

When searching for ascending triangles, look for minor highs close together (weeks apart, but usually not months between tops) that peak near the same price. Then look directly below those peaks to see if the valleys trend upward following a straight line.

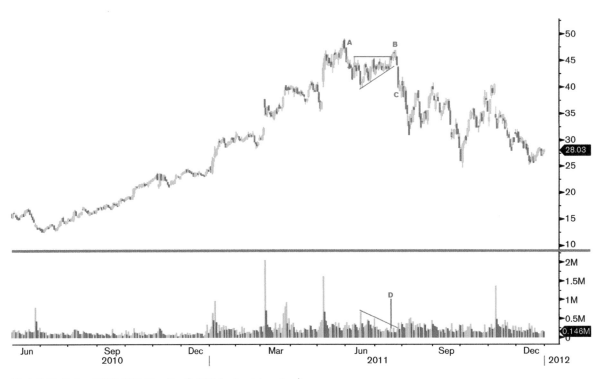

Exhibit 8.1: LXU US Equity (LSB Industries Inc)

Sometimes I will see an up-sloping line of valleys following a trend. Then I look above them and see a horizontal line of peaks. That combination spells triangle.

The accompanying table lists the important characteristics of ascending triangles.

Characteristic	Discussion
Horizontal top line	Price along the top follows a horizontal trend.
Up-sloping bottom line	Price makes a series of higher valleys, following a trendline. The two trendlines converge.

Characteristic	Discussion
Price crossing	Price must cross the pattern from side to side, filling the triangle with movement. Avoid patterns with excessive white space in the center of the triangle.
Volume	Volume in the pattern recedes and can be especially low the day before the breakout.
Breakout	Can be in any direction, but is upward the majority of the time.

Price along the top of the ascending triangle follows a horizontal or nearly horizontal trendline. Along the bottom, the minor lows bounce off an up-sloping trendline drawn connecting them.

Look at Exhibit 8.2.

Minor highs A through D stop near the same price. Minor lows E through G touch the bottom trendline. Together they form an ascending triangle, only this one has a downward breakout.

Make sure that price crosses the chart pattern plenty of times. What you do not want to see is white space in the middle of the pattern. I show an example of that later in this chapter.

Volume tends to recede over the life of the triangle, but that varies from triangle to triangle. The chart shows volume trending higher in the first half of the pattern and then downward leading to the breakout. Do not discard an ascending triangle simply because of an abnormal volume trend.

The breakout from an ascending triangle can be in any direction, but is usually upward.

This is another example of a busted ascending triangle. Price breaks out downward and does not drop far (less than 10 percent) before reversing and closing above the top of the triangle. When that happens, it busts the downward breakout.

Unfortunately, this bust did not result in a tasty move upward. That might be because of the extended rise leading to the triangle. In fact, the downward breakout was a clue to weakness to begin with.

Ascending Triangle Psychology

In ascending triangles, price peaks for the same reason it does in rectangles: Traders sell when the stock reaches their target price.

Suppose that Molly runs a mutual fund and wants to sell several hundred thousand shares of ABC Chewing Gum. Every time the stock reaches $35, she sells some. Her selling creates a ceiling on the stock.

Harry runs the trading department of a hedge fund, and he loves ABC Chewing. When the stock drops to 30, he buys as many shares as he can, but the stock runs away from him and becomes too expensive to chase.

Johnny is a rich swing trader. He watches Mutual Fund Molly create overhead resistance at 35 and sees Hedge Fund Harry put a floor in the stock at 30.

KEY POINT:

When searching for ascending triangles, make sure price crosses the chart pattern from side to side several times. Price should not be bunched up near the start nor near the end with an empty white hole in the middle.

KEY POINT:

An ascending triangle forms because of increasing demand at lower prices matched with selling at a constant price.

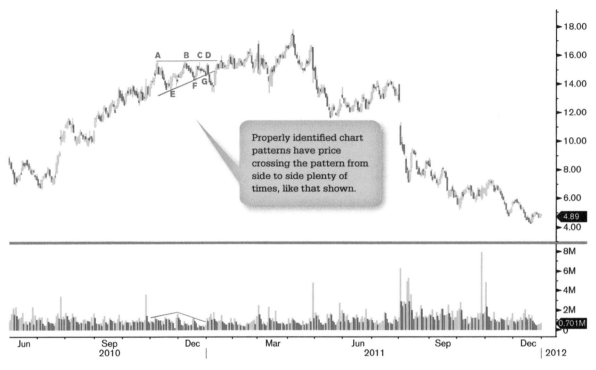

Properly identified chart patterns have price crossing the pattern from side to side plenty of times, like that shown.

Exhibit 8.2: FOE US Equity (Ferro Corp)

When the stock drops to 30.25, he starts buying, knowing that he can probably sell when it approaches 35. "Easy money," he says and smiles.

Harry sees volume tick up and believes that others are buying ahead of him. He raises his buy price to 30.50 and starts eating as many shares as he can before they disappear from his plate.

On the next cycle, Harry has to raise his buy price to 31 to stay ahead of the other cannibals. The hunt continues until Molly sells all of her shares or Harry bags his quota and quits. When one side gives up, the other side yells, "Tag! You're it!" and snatches the stock; then a breakout ensues, ending the pattern.

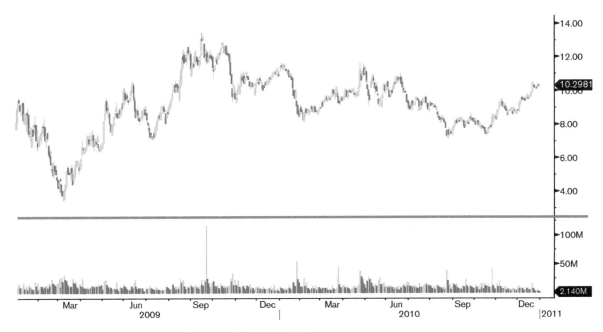

Exhibit 8.7: CX US Equity (Cemex SAB de CV)

Exhibit 8.8 reveals the locations of these chart patterns.

Hopefully, you were able to pick out the ascending triangles in February and April.

The next chapter discusses descending triangles. Think of them as ascending triangles who forgot to refill their anti-depressant medication.

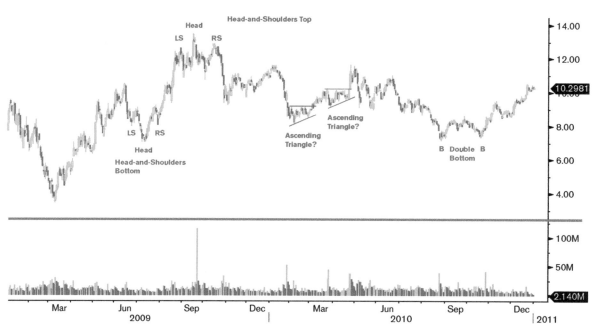

Exhibit 8.8: CX US Equity (Cemex SAB de CV)

Test Yourself

Answer these questions with true or false.

1. The bottom trendline of an ascending triangle has a horizontal slope.
2. The top trendline can slant, but not too much.
3. The apex is where the trendlines converge.
4. Directly above or below the triangle apex is a likely turning point.
5. Ascending triangles break out upward most of the time.

Answers: 1. False; 2. True; 3. True; 4. True; 5. True

CHAPTER 9

Descending Triangles

Descending triangles share characteristics of their ascending brothers including one horizontal trendline and another sloping.

Exhibit 9.1 shows two examples in red.

Starting in May, the stock drops like a Texas hailstone and slams into support at A, bounces several times and forms a descending triangle.

Points A, B, and C highlight valleys that align along a horizontal bottom trendline. Along the top, peaks D, E, and F touch another line, but this one slopes downward. The two trendlines merge at the triangle's apex.

Volume trends downward (G) until spiking on the breakout day, and that behavior is typical of many chart patterns.

Be still my heart: This is an example of a trading setup that I love. Price breaks out downward but

reverses, pushes upward, and closes above the top of the triangle. When it does that, it busts the pattern. Busted patterns can lead to good performance, as this example shows.

I was hesitant to show triangle H because the bottom trendline, although shown flat, is probably better drawn sloping upward. If you redraw it, the pattern becomes a symmetrical triangle, the subject of the next chapter. However, the bottoms are close enough to the trendline that the pattern qualifies as a descending triangle, too.

Identification Guidelines

The following table lists the important characteristics that help identify descending triangles.

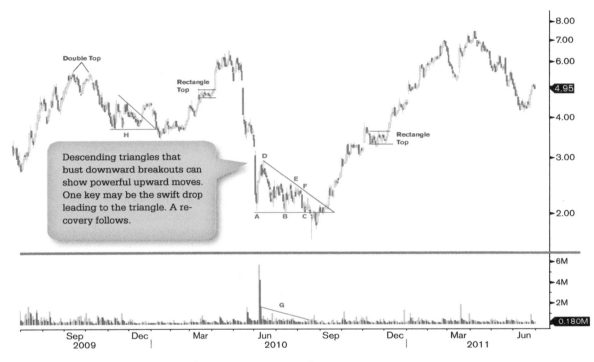

Descending triangles that bust downward breakouts can show powerful upward moves. One key may be the swift drop leading to the triangle. A recovery follows.

Exhibit 9.1: NWY US Equity (New York & Co Inc)

Characteristic	Discussion
Horizontal bottom line	Price along the bottom follows a horizontal trend.
Down-sloping top line	Price along the top slopes downward, following a trendline.
Price crossing	Price must cross the pattern from side to side, filling the triangle with movement. Avoid patterns with excessive white space in the center of the triangle.
Volume	Volume in the pattern recedes and can be especially low the day before the breakout.
Breakout	Can be in any direction, but is downward the majority of the time.

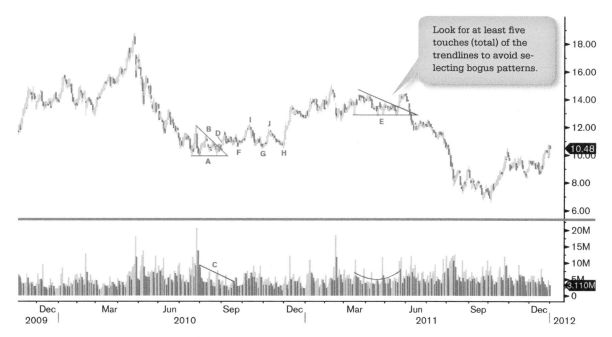

Look for at least five touches (total) of the trendlines to avoid selecting bogus patterns.

Exhibit 9.2: MAS US Equity (Masco Corp)

To help explain the guidelines, look at Exhibit 9.2.

The bottom of triangle A shows three touches of a horizontal trendline. The valleys do not bottom at exactly the same price, but they come close. They *look* as if they belong on the same trendline.

Along the top, B, another trendline connects peaks that form at successively lower levels and yet still touch the trendline. I look for three touches along the diagonal if only two touch the bottom. That is a safety measure to prevent selecting triangles that are just random squiggles on the price chart.

Price crosses the triangle from side to side, leaving no room for white space. This is another important safety tip to avoid selecting bogus patterns.

Volume typically recedes in the chart pattern, but do not discard a descending triangle just because the volume pattern shows increasing volume. Triangle E has U-shaped volume and yet it is a valid descending triangle.

Price can break out of a descending triangle in any direction, but most often, it will be downward.

Look at points F through J. Is this a descending triangle? Yes. I dislike only two touches on the top, and

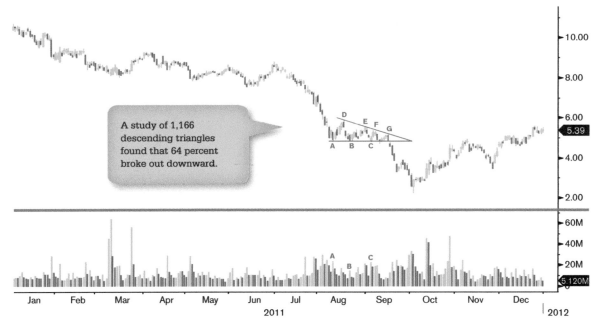

A study of 1,166 descending triangles found that 64 percent broke out downward.

Exhibit 9.3: CX US Equity (Cemex SAB de CV)

the bottom trendline could be straighter, but the combination works.

There is another descending triangle on the chart that is not marked. Where is it? Go look for it before I tell you where it is.

Hint: Look on the far left of the chart.

In mid-November 2009, the stock began forming a descending triangle that extended to early January, breaking out upward. It has three touches on the top and three on the bottom.

Descending Triangle Psychology

Suppose you are a large institutional investor that wants to own Cemex, pictured in Exhibit 9.3, at $5 a share.

When the stock drops to $5, you buy (A). Notice the associated rise in volume.

I watch the ticker tape and see large blocks roll across my screen at $5 and below, so I conduct research and discover that the stock represents a compelling value. I buy too. Together, along with other buyers, we send the price moving up.

When the stock hits $6, I dump the turkey, pass Go, and collect my $200. Other sellers that view it as overvalued decide to cash in as well (D).

This selling pressure causes price to ease lower and eventually trigger more buying at a lower price (B). When the stock rises, those that missed selling as the stock approached $6 sell now.

The cycle of buying and selling continues at E, C, F, and G. At G, well into the traditional worst performing month of the year (September), selling pressure increases, overwhelming buying demand, forcing the stock to push through support. The stock tumbles.

The footprint that remains on the chart outlines a descending triangle.

Variations

Look at Exhibit 9.4 because it reveals a flaw in pattern identification.

Price anchors the bottom of the chart pattern at A and B with minor low trendline touches at the same price. Along the top, price touches the trendline multiple times on the way to C. The peak at C pokes up through the top of the triangle, staging a breakout.

What is wrong with this triangle? It contains too much white space in the middle of the pattern. Price

does not cross the triangle from side to side, filling the chart pattern with price movement.

If you look at the blue inset, with the triangle boundaries removed, you can see that this is nothing more than the stock climbing to a peak and withdrawing. It is not a triangle.

Compare pattern ABC with the one in the red inset at D. The D triangle shows plenty of price crossings as well as trendline touches spaced throughout the triangle. Image D is how a descending triangle should look.

Exercise

You will likely have difficulty finding a descending triangle in Exhibit 9.5. Here is a hint: Look for the down-sloping trendline first. You should also find a double bottom. Another hint? Both are large patterns.

The next chart (see Exhibit 9.6) reveals the descending triangle. It has three touches on the top and two on the bottom. Price crosses the pattern and fills the white space, but because the triangle is so large, it may look like too much white space. It takes time for price to cross the pattern, so it is fine.

Notice that the double bottom shares the triangle's space. Both are valid chart patterns.

I think that the next exercise is easy, but then I know where to look. You will find a descending triangle, two double tops, one double bottom, and a

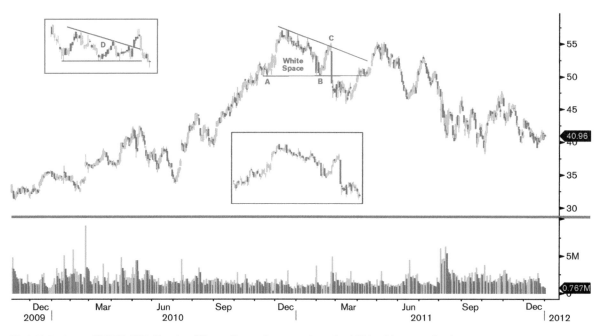

Exhibit 9.4: EXPD US Equity (Expeditors International of Washington Inc)

symmetrical triangle. Try to find as many of those as you can. (See Exhibit 9.7.)

The descending triangle is at A, in red. Price touches each trendline, forming a beautiful wedge shape. It reminds me of the rubber doorstop I use to keep the wind from slamming the door shut in summer. (See Exhibit 9.8.)

You probably did not select triangle B, and that is good because it is not a descending triangle. There is too much white space between the trendlines to qualify this as a valid triangle.

On the right of the chart is a symmetrical triangle. It is a more complicated shape, with two converging trendlines. Unlike ascending and descending triangles, the shape of the pattern does not hint at the breakout direction. Symmetrical triangles are as plentiful as fleas on a dog, and can be just as annoying. They are the subject of the next chapter.

Test Yourself

Answer these statements with true or false.

1. An *ascending* triangle has a horizontal top trendline.
2. A descending triangle has a down-sloping top trendline.
3. At least four touches, total, of the two trendlines is required, but five or more is better.

Answers: 1. True; 2. True; 3. True

CHAPTER 10

Symmetrical Triangles

Symmetrical triangles take pattern recognition to a new level. We ditch horizontal trendlines and use diagonal ones to outline the pattern.

Exhibit 10.1 shows a pair of symmetrical triangles swimming in a price sea. They remind me of angelfish I had in my 55-gallon aquarium when I lived near Boston.

I like the red triangle at C. Price touches two sloping trendlines that merge at the triangle apex. Directly above the apex, in this example, is a price peak. I have mentioned this apex and turning behavior before because it works well and gives traders a clue where the trend might shift.

Notice that the blue triangle apex (D) sits beneath peak E. It is not as timely (it comes late as price is about to slide) as the other triangle's prediction, but it is valuable, too.

Triangle D cuts through price on both trendlines, so it is not ideal. Volume trends lower as it does in many symmetrical triangles.

Identification Guidelines

The following table lists important characteristics that help identify symmetrical triangles.

Characteristic	Discussion
Two sloping and converging trendlines	Price follows two sloping trendlines that join at the triangle apex.
Price crossing	Price must cross the pattern from side to side, filling the triangle with movement. Avoid patterns with excessive white space in the center of the triangle.
Volume	Volume in the pattern recedes and can be especially low the day before the breakout.

KEY POINT:
A symmetrical triangle appears like an angelfish bounded by two converging trendlines. The breakout can be in any direction.

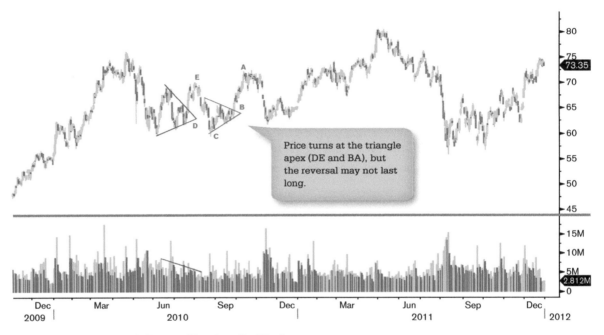

Exhibit 10.1: BA US Equity (Boeing Co/The)

Characteristic	Discussion
Breakout	Can be in any direction.
Duration	Should be longer than three weeks; otherwise they could be pennants.

To help explain the guidelines, look at Exhibit 10.2.

This is an example of a large symmetrical triangle at C, bounded by red trendlines. Price touches each trendline three times (twice is a minimum, but I like to see three) in distinct minor highs and minor lows. As price crosses the chart pattern from side to side, it fills the white space. Since this is a large example, do not expect price to fill the entire area. White space will be present, but should not look like a cavity too large for a dentist to fill.

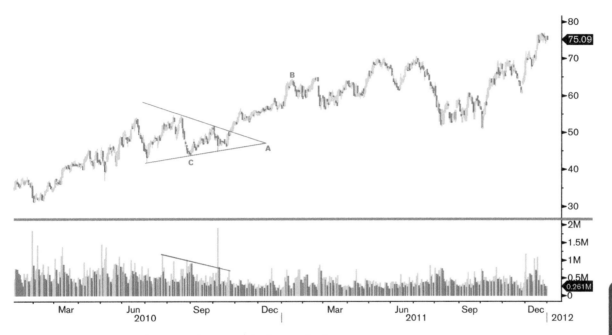

Exhibit 10.2: ALK US Equity (Alaska Air Group Inc)

Volume recedes, but is often irregular looking. Do not discard a symmetrical triangle because the volume pattern is wrong.

The breakout can be in any direction, including horizontal where price oozes out the front of the triangle.

Most symmetrical triangles should be longer than three weeks to help distinguish them from pennants. The exception is when a pennant is missing a flagpole.

In that case, the pennant is really a small symmetrical triangle.

Symmetrical Triangle Psychology

Symmetrical triangles are the epitome of confusion. Price does not know which way to trend. Exhibit 10.3 shows another example of a symmetrical triangle.

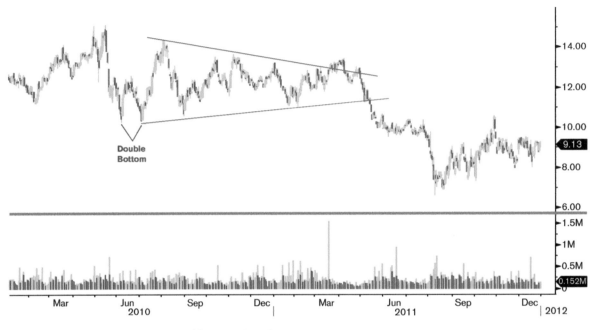

Exhibit 10.3: GFF US Equity (Griffon Corp)

At the start of the pattern, bulls push price up in the hopes that the double bottom will confirm as a valid chart pattern. That means price must close above the highest peak between the two bottoms, which it does.

The straight-line run continues until meeting overhead resistance set up by bears wanting to dump the stock at a price they believe is too rich.

Their selling forces price back down. When it approaches the price level of the prior minor low, eager bulls who missed their opportunity to buy do so now. Others may add to existing positions. That buying demand pushes price up until meeting bears wanting to take profits.

The oscillations continue, with bears taking profits earlier and bulls buying sooner, tightening the coil. Eventually, buying demand outpaces selling pressure and the coil releases, springing upward in this example.

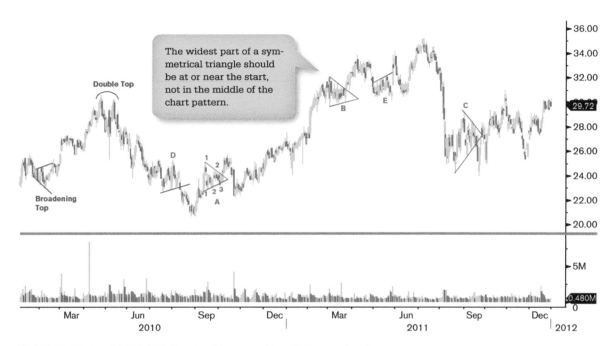

The widest part of a symmetrical triangle should be at or near the start, not in the middle of the chart pattern.

Exhibit 10.4: ASNA US Equity (Ascena Retail Group Inc.)

Almost as soon as that happens, the bears regroup and force price back down, and they keep selling until the stock bottoms in August. What remains on the chart is a long symmetrical triangle.

Variations

Exhibit 10.4 shows several chart patterns, including some that hint of being symmetrical triangles, but are not.

Look at triangle A. What attracts me are the three touches of the bottom trendline. However, the top shows only two touches. That is not optimum.

Triangle B is flawed because erasing the first touch on the bottom makes the line horizontal (but it may be difficult to see).

The top of triangle C is near the middle of the chart pattern instead of the start, making it difficult to approve as

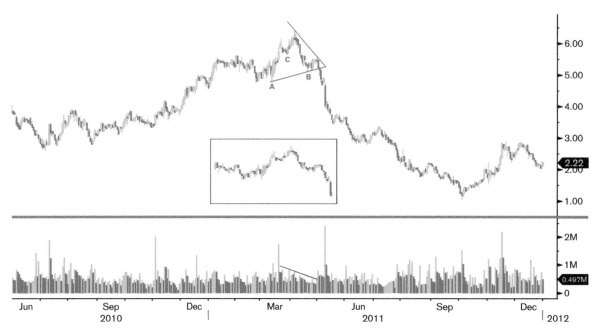

Exhibit 10.5: HW US Equity (Headwaters Inc)

a valid triangle, too. Nevertheless, all three qualify as symmetrical triangles even though none is perfect.

Now look at pattern D. Along the bottom is an upsloping trendline with three touches. Peak D is in the middle of the pattern. Using D as the start of the triangle would make it look too lopsided, too unbalanced. It is not a symmetrical triangle.

Confused? If any chart pattern looks questionable, look for another one. They are as plentiful as ants at a picnic.

Pattern E has many touches along the peaks, but too much white space on the bottom. It is not a symmetrical triangle.

Exhibit 10.5 gives a warning of how not to draw a symmetrical triangle.

Price along the bottom touches points A and B, widely separated. Along the top are two minor high touches.

Look at C. The white space is obvious. This is not a symmetrical triangle. It is just a peak with red lines

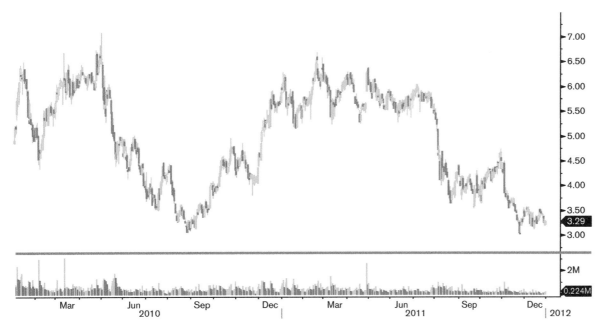

Exhibit 10.6: MEA US Equity (Metalico Inc)

drawn to resemble one. The inset shows the peak without the lines.

Exercise

In Exhibit 10.6, I found three symmetrical triangles, two double tops, and a head-and-shoulders top, but no partridge in a pear tree. See if you can find the chart patterns as well.

Exhibit 10.7 shows the answers. The symmetrical triangle at A is the easiest to find, probably

because it is large with so many trendline touches.

Triangle B is harder to spot because the top spike upward at the start might not register as a minor high touch. Without it, the pattern would resemble an ascending triangle.

Triangle C is the hardest to find. It seems buried in an area where price is directionless. There are three touches along the top trendline, but only two along the bottom. Notice that D does not qualify as a

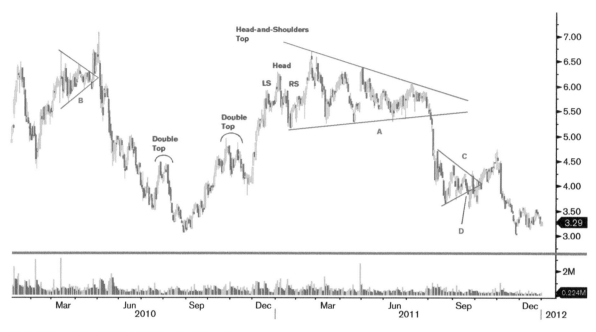

Exhibit 10.7: MEA US Equity (Metalico Inc)

touch since it is not a minor low. D is part of a straight-line run downward that just happens to gap where the trendline touches.

Exhibit 10.8 has three symmetrical triangles. Also look for a descending triangle, head-and-shoulders bottom, and Big W, which is a type of double bottom with tall sides.

Exhibit 10.9 shows the answers. If you picked A as a symmetrical triangle, be careful because candle

A is not a minor low and should not be used to anchor the start of the pattern. However, the pattern does appear wedge shaped. It is a symmetrical triangle.

Triangle B is large with plenty of trendline touches and should have been easy to spot.

Point C is the same height as D. That means the down-sloping trendline does not quite touch C. Even so, I think it is fine as a symmetrical triangle.

CHAPTER 11

Flags and Pennants

Pennants remind me of those pointed streamers that line roped-off areas at festivals. They are the same as flags except that the trendlines bounding the pattern converge. In flags, they are parallel.

Exhibit 11.1 shows a sprinkling of flags and pennants.

Let us start with pennant B. This is the kind of pennant that traders dream about. The trend begins at A in a straight-line run up to the pennant (B). Price consolidates, forming a triangle shape (the pennant). After that, price resumes a strong move up to C. The AB move is about the same as BC. Thus, the pennant can act as a half-staff pattern; it can appear midway in a price trend. The same is true of flags and other chart patterns, too.

C is another pennant. Unlike B, where price moved sideways in the pennant, this one has a more traditional slope—downward against the trend.

Pennant D, on the far right of the chart, looks like a small version of a descending triangle, a pattern that has a flat bottom and down-sloping top.

Flags have parallel trendlines whereas pennants converge. The flags appear in blue, but not because they have been holding their breath like a child throwing a tantrum.

Identification Guidelines

The following table lists important characteristics to help identify flags and pennants. For such simple patterns, why does it seem so complicated?

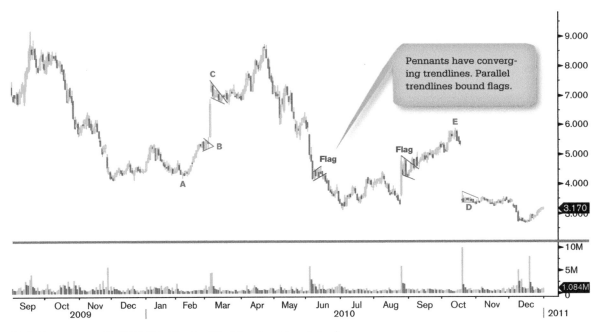

Exhibit 11.1: CWTR US Equity (Coldwater Creek Inc)

Characteristic	Discussion
Price trends	Flags and pennants always rest upon a flagpole, so look for a strong price run leading to them.
Two converging trendlines	For flags, price follows two parallel or nearly parallel trendlines. For pennants, price follows two converging trendlines.
Volume	Volume in the pattern recedes.
Breakout	Can be in any direction.
Duration	Flags and pennants are shorter than three weeks.

Flags and pennants must have flagpoles.

Exhibit 11.2: ABFS US Equity (Arkansas Best Corp)

The easiest way to find a flag or pennant is to begin with the flagpole. Look for a straight-line price run. Price will consolidate along that run. When it does, it can take the shape of a flag or pennant.

To help explain the guidelines, look at Exhibit 11.2.

The flag pattern begins with the flagpole, AB. If a strong trend (a straight-line price run) does not exist, then look elsewhere. Atop the pole, price consolidates and forms flag BC. After that, price breaks out downward

(C) and drops, pulling back briefly at D, but then powering down to the launch price and digging a crater (E).

Flags should form between two parallel or nearly parallel trendlines. The two lines do not have to be exactly parallel. Pennants should form between two converging trendlines. For both flags and pennants, trendline touch count is not important.

Price in the flag or pennant can slope in any direction, including sideways, but is usually against the

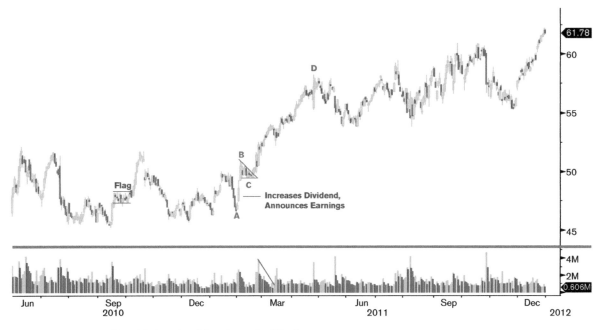

Exhibit 11.3: HSY US Equity (Hershey Co/The)

prevailing trend. In this case, the trend is up from A to B and the flag slopes down from B to C.

Volume typically recedes in a flag or pennant just as it does in many other chart patterns. The breakout can be in any direction, too, but usually follows the trend leading to the flag or pennant.

Flags and pennants are short, no longer than three weeks. This is an arbitrary value. What you are looking for is a small knot of congestion in a strong price run. Once the knot unties (breaks out), price should continue on its way.

Flag F is notable because it rests in the middle of the GH move.

Flag and Pennant Psychology

Exhibit 11.3 highlights one pennant and one flag.

At A, the smart money began buying, believing or knowing that a good earnings report was coming.

Two days later, the company announced earnings and raised their outlook to the top end of the target range while increasing the dividend.

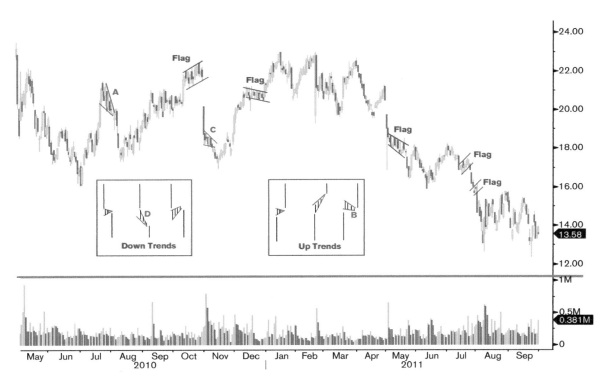

Exhibit 11.4: CKP US Equity (Checkpoint Systems Inc)

Buying demand propelled the stock higher like an overly excited kid gobbling Halloween candy. Then the bears returned to the trading table and started a food fight with the bulls. The fight between evenly matched opponents pushed price sideways, forming the pennant. This one had a flat base and down-sloping top, suggesting a group of investors wanted to buy the stock at a set price (49.50) but stopped buying when price climbed too high. Their buying put a floor underneath the stock.

After the bears digested the news and ran for the exits, the bulls took over and sent the stock moving higher again, rising from C to D. Notice how one good earnings report can launch a stock toward the heavens. Or maybe it was the candy.

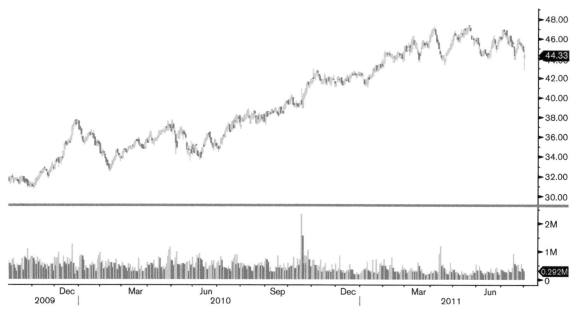

Exhibit 11.5: NST US Equity (NSTAR)

Variations

Exhibit 11.4 shows five flags (blue) and two pennants (red) with four additional variations in the inset. Although the insets show pennants, use your creative mind to redraw the pennant trendlines as parallel lines for flag variations.

Pennant A forms after a mediocre uptrend. I would call it powerful if price broke out of the pennant upward, but it does not. Rather, the pennant slopes downward, which is typical, but then price continues down, oozing out the end of the pennant like caulking. That configuration follows pattern B (except for a downward breakout, of course).

Pennant C forms after price gaps lower. The pennant boundary is irregular in shape, but highlights a small congestion region where price gathers its strength for the coming drop. That drop occurs, completing the configuration like that shown at D.

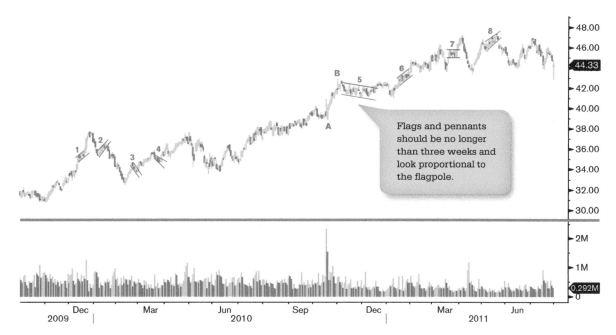

Exhibit 11.6: NST US Equity (NSTAR)

In the two insets, I show various pennant shapes in up and down trends. Be aware that pennants can break out in any direction, so expect that. I show only the patterns acting as continuations of the prevailing price trend and not reversals.

Exercise

Exhibit 11.5 has a multitude of flags. Try to find as many as you can that obey the identification guidelines discussed earlier. I found eight and stopped there. One is large and may not qualify. That is a hint, of course.

Exhibit 11.6 shows the answers. I numbered the flags, making them easier to see. Flag 5 is the likely offender to the three-week rule. It is about a month long. That would still be fine if the flagpole were long, too. Strong and long trends tend to precede extended sideways movement. This flag has the extended sideways movement, but the flagpole height is unexciting.

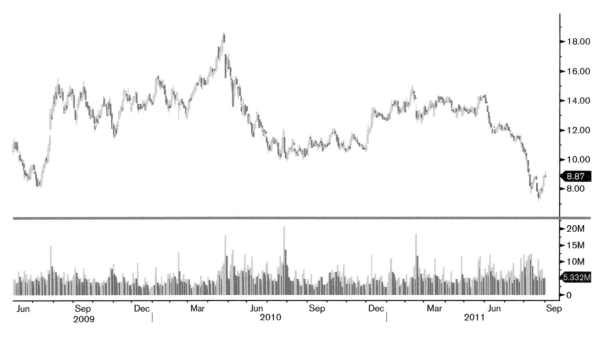

Exhibit 11.7: MAS US Equity (Masco Corp)

In other words, the flag or pennant should be pro-portional to the height of the flagpole. This pole begins at A and ends at B, which looks too short for the flag.

Are you rested enough to try again? Exhibit 11.7 shows pennants. Find as many as you can.

Hint: I found five.

Exhibit 11.8 shows the answers. Starting from the left at A, price begins trending to pennant B, breaking out upward and ending at C. The trend start (A) is im-portant when the pennant acts as a half-staff pattern, as in this case.

The rise from D to E matches the decline from E to F, only EF takes more time.

Pennant G is perhaps the prettiest on the chart. The trend begins at F and goes to H. The stock, from the bottom of G to H, only climbs about half the FG move.

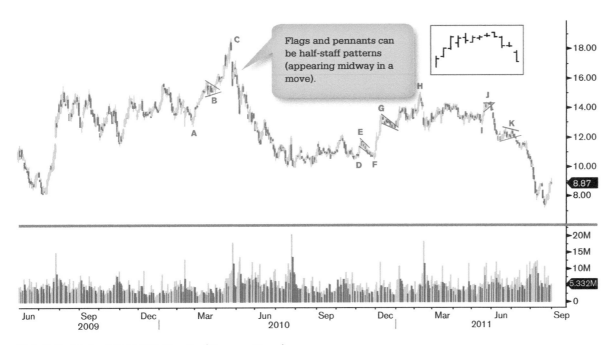

Flags and pennants can be half-staff patterns (appearing midway in a move).

Exhibit 11.8: MAS US Equity (Masco Corp)

You may argue that J is a flag and not a pennant, so I show the price action in the inset. The pattern resembles a small ascending triangle, but due to its size, becomes a pennant.

Pennant K is large and loose looking. Price meanders up and down within its boundaries. The straight-line run down from J looks proportional to the pennant size.

The next chapter shifts the focus from drawing trendlines to finding potholes that bottom near the same price. We call them double bottoms.

Test Yourself

Answer these statements with true or false.

1. One pennant variation happens when parallel trendlines form the pennant.
2. A pennant must have a flagpole; otherwise, it is not a pennant.
3. Pennants always appear midway in a strong price trend.
4. Since the duration of a flag has a maximum of three weeks, it appears only on the daily or intraday charts.
5. In a flag, price most often slants against the prevailing price trend.
6. A flag without a flagpole is like peanut butter without jelly (meaning they go together).
7. The flag and pennant size should be proportional to the flagpole length.

Answers: 1. False; 2. True; 3. False; 4. False; 5. True; 6. True; 7. True

a shock, so you sit paralyzed and just watch it weekly, wondering if the slide is over.

Eventually it bottoms at A, but you wait because you are not sure the decline has ended. When you look again, the stock has climbed too far to chase, despite the power of your hunting rifle.

At E, you vow that if the stock ever returns to the price level of A, you will bag it. The stock cooperates, reaching B. You shoot and score some shares!

Others do the same, putting a floor on the stock. Price rises, eventually confirming the twin valley pattern as a valid double bottom.

Who actually hunts like that? I do. I bought at 39.72 on June 3 (B) and sold it at 54 a year later, pocketing a 5.4 percent dividend along the way.

Variations

Double bottoms have several variations and Exhibit 12.4 shows three of them.

Pattern A is called an Eve & Eve double bottom. B is an Eve & Adam, and C is an Adam & Adam double bottom.

The difference between Adam and Eve is the shape of the bottom. Adam bottoms are thin, narrow price spikes, often composed of a single day or two. Eve is wider and more rounded looking. If Eve has price spikes, they are more numerous and stubby.

Eve bottoms tend to be wide and widen out as price climbs. Adam bottoms tend to remain narrow.

For example, look at the width of Eve at B. The two vertical red lines at D show how it widens out. Compare that to the Adam bottom at E. The lines remain narrow.

I often use the width of the bottom in this manner to determine whether I am looking at an Eve or Adam bottom.

Another way to determine the type is to ask if the two bottoms look alike. If so, then you have Adam & Adam or Eve & Eve. Otherwise, it is a mix of the two: Eve & Adam or Adam & Eve.

Why the emphasis on Adam and Eve? Because the various types perform differently.

Exhibit 12.5 shows the last two variations.

An Adam & Eve double bottom appears in February and it has a narrow bottom (three days wide) followed by a wide one. The chart pattern confirms as a valid double bottom when price closes above the peak between the two valleys.

The other double bottom variation is probably one you have never heard of. I call it an ugly double bottom. Price bottoms at A and then bounces to form a higher bottom, B (at least 5 percent higher, by the way). When price confirms the chart pattern by closing above the peak between the two bottoms, it indicates that the trend has changed from down to up.

Exercise

Find as many valid double bottoms as you can in Exhibit 12.6. Do not concern yourself with any of

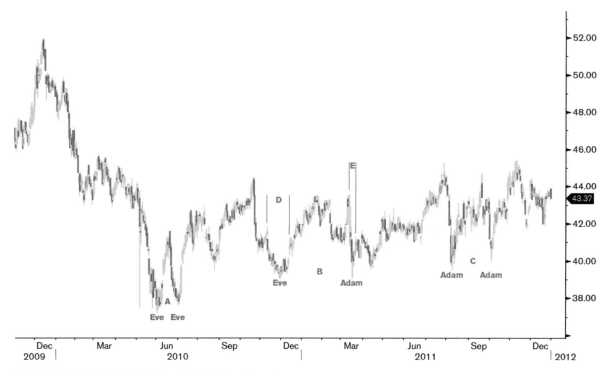

Exhibit 12.4: EXC US Equity (Exelon Corp)

the identification guideline numbers, such as two to seven weeks between bottoms, or 5 percent apart, and so on. Just look for two valleys that bottom at or near the same price and confirm as valid patterns. Do not look for ugly double bottoms, and do not worry about the Adam and Eve variations. Also pretend that the long green downward spike in May does not exist.

Exhibit 12.7 shows what I found. First, in the lower right of the chart is the only valid double bottom, AB. Price confirms it when the stock closes above the top of the pattern, at C.

If you marked DE, that would be wrong because it does not confirm.

Bottom FG confirms, but it is not a bottom. Price must trend downward into the chart pattern, not rise up

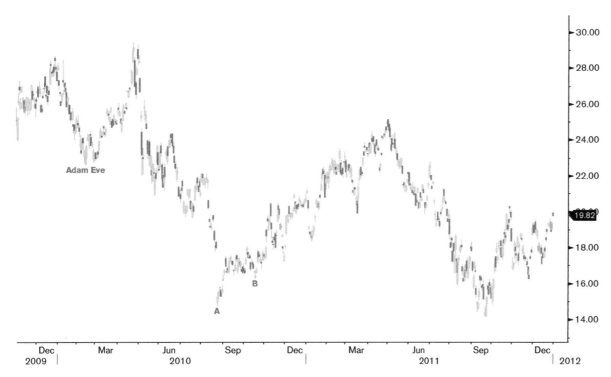

Exhibit 12.5: CRH US Equity (CRH PLC)

from the grave. The rule I use is that in-bound price must be higher than the peak in the middle of the double bottom to guarantee that it is indeed trending down into the chart pattern. That does not occur on the FG bottom.

Confused? I explain it again in the next chapter.

All of the other potential double bottoms on the chart have one or both of those flaws. They do not confirm or are located in an uptrend.

Exhibit 12.8 has multiple double bottoms in it. Find as many as you can, but do not look for those narrower than about two weeks and forget about ugly double bottoms, too.

Exhibit 12.9 shows the answers. I drew a line connecting the bottoms for your viewing pleasure. Bottom A confirms as a valid pattern in a downward price trend. If you excluded it because the two valleys

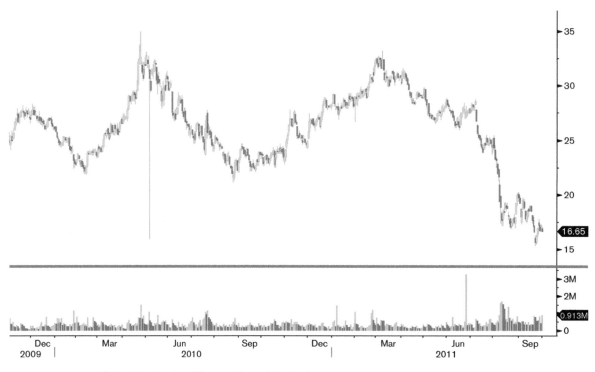

Exhibit 12.6: EXP US Equity (Eagle Materials Inc)

did not bottom at the same price (they are 72 cents apart or 1.7 percent), then, good. I still consider it one.

G is one of those double bottoms I told you not to worry about because the valleys are too narrow. If you found it anyway, wonderful! It is a double bottom. Price makes a third bottom, but that happens after the double bottom confirms.

B, D, and E should have been easy (maybe C, too). E is especially delicious since the Eve bottom is so much wider than Adam.

What about bottom F? That is not a double bottom. Why? Look at bottoms 1 and 2. They do not confirm until *after* bottom 3 forms. This is an example of a triple bottom, the subject of our next chapter.

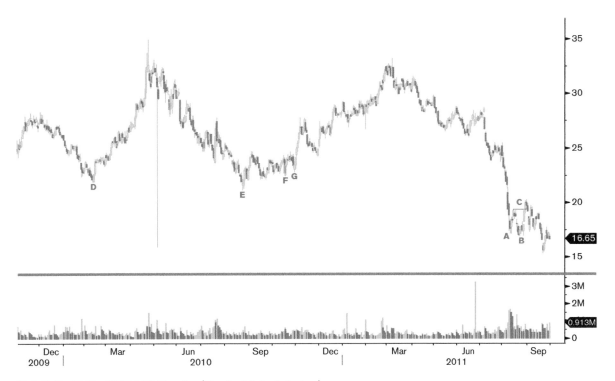

Exhibit 12.7: EXP US Equity (Eagle Materials Inc)

If you found bottoms 2 and 3, you should have looked to the left and found bottom 1, again, forming a triple bottom.

By now, you probably hate me. Are you going to remove me from your will? Do that after you die, and after you read the next chapter on triple bottoms.

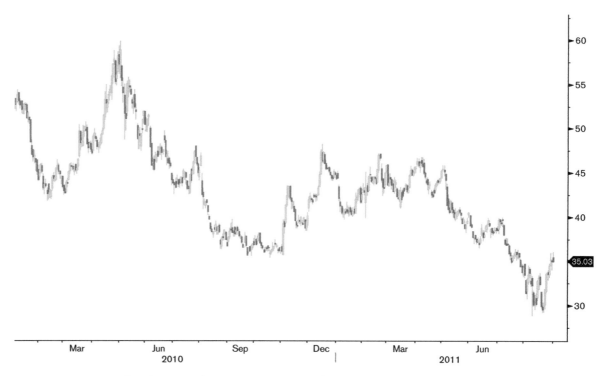

Exhibit 12.8: VMC US Equity (Vulcan Materials Co)

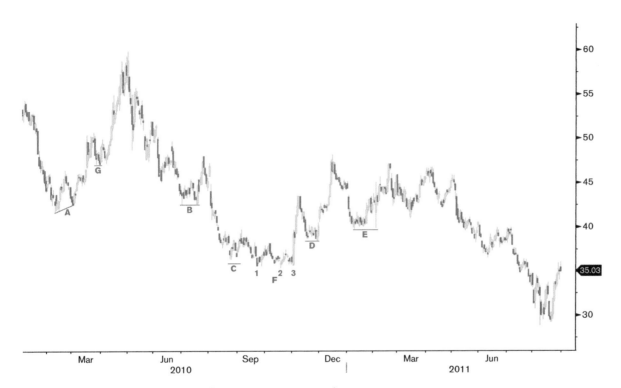

Exhibit 12.9: VMC US Equity (Vulcan Materials Co)

Test Yourself

Answer true or false to the following statements.

1. A double bottom is just squiggles on a price chart until it confirms.

2. Confirmation of a double bottom is when price rises at least 10 percent above the lowest bottom.

3. Price must trend down into a double bottom.

4. The peak between the two bottoms should rise at least 10 percent above the lowest bottom, but if it does not, who cares?

5. If price closes below the lowest bottom before confirming the double bottom, it invalidates the chart pattern.

Answers: 1. True; 2. False; 3. True; 4. True; 5. True

CHAPTER 13

Triple Bottoms

Now that we have trained ourselves to find two bottoms that line up at the same price, let us look for triplets: three bottoms in a row. It is as easy as it sounds, except that triple bottoms are sometimes confused with head-and-shoulders bottoms. Maybe it is not so easy . . .

Triple bottoms are considerably rarer than double bottoms, but the technique used to find them is the same. Find a double bottom and then look to the left and right to see if a third bottom exists at the same price.

Exhibit 13.1 shows an example.

Based on what you have learned in this book, which of the three patterns are triple bottoms (guess)?

Look at bottom ABC. Price trends downward into the chart pattern. If you do not see a downward price trend, then it is not a bottom reversal. The pattern has three price spikes, with A slightly above the other two. Price confirms the pattern by *closing* above the highest peak between the three bottoms.

It is a triple bottom.

DEF is similar to ABC in that two of three bottoms are near the same price. However, F is much higher than DE so this would work better as double bottom DE with throwback F.

HIJ has a center valley (I) below the other two. That is a dead giveaway. It is a head-and-shoulders bottom, a chart pattern I will be discussing later in the book (see Chapter 16).

Identification Guidelines

What is involved in identifying triple bottoms? You can probably guess most of them, but the following table provides a list.

Characteristic	Discussion
Downward price trend	The short-term price trend leading to the triple bottom is down.

> **KEY POINT:**
>
> Triple bottoms are three valleys that bottom near the same price. The chart pattern acts as a bullish reversal of the downward price trend.

> **KEY POINT:**
>
> Price must *trend* downward into a bottom and upward into a top. That trend is what qualifies the chart pattern as a bottom or top, respectively. Without the trend, then you do not have a reversal pattern.

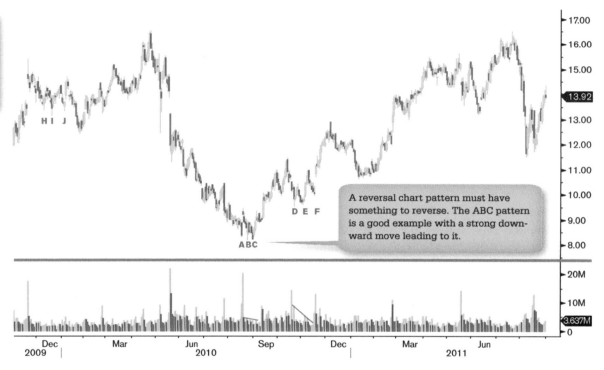

A reversal chart pattern must have something to reverse. The ABC pattern is a good example with a strong downward move leading to it.

Exhibit 13.1: CHS US Equity (Chico's FAS Inc)

Characteristic	Discussion
Three bottoms	Three minor lows are involved in a triple bottom. Sometimes they can be one-day price spikes or wider, more rounded turns. Each valley tends to look similar to the others.
Same price	Each minor low should bottom *near* the same price. Rarely will all three bottom at exactly the same price, so be flexible.
Volume	Volume recedes, meaning it is higher on the left than the right, but each bottom can show significant volume. Do not exclude a pattern because it has an unusual volume shape.
Confirmation	Price must confirm the triple bottom by closing above the highest peak between the three bottoms.

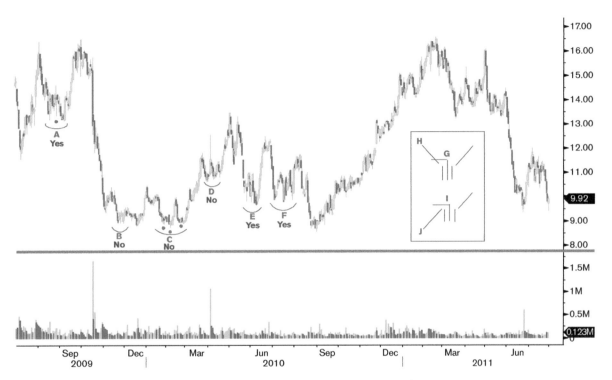

Exhibit 13.5: PMTI US Equity (Palomar Medical Technologies Inc)

Pattern F also has a lower middle valley but if this were a person, he would have the nickname "No neck." It is a valid triple bottom and not a head-and-shoulders bottom.

Exercise

To test what you have learned in this chapter, the first exercise (see Exhibit 13.6) is easy. There are only four patterns on the chart that I want to highlight. Two are triple bottoms and two are head-and-shoulders bottoms. See if you can find all of them even though we have not yet covered the head-and-shoulders.

Exhibit 13.7 shows the answers.

A and B are the triple bottoms. They exist in a downward price trend, form three bottoms near the same price, and confirm when price closes above

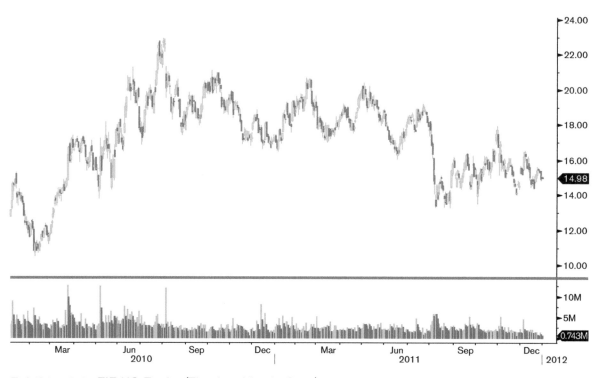

Exhibit 13.6: TIE US Equity (Titanium Metals Corp)

the highest peak between the three valleys in each pattern.

The two head-and-shoulders bottoms would be difficult to confuse as triple bottoms since the heads are much lower than the surrounding valleys.

This next exercise (see Exhibit 13.8) is trickier than the last one. Look for three triple bottoms and one head-and-shoulders bottom.

Exhibit 13.9 shows the answers. Triple bottom A has a right bottom below the other two, but it still acts as a reversal of the downward price run. Price on the right valley does not sink too far below (just 20 cents) the other two to invalidate the triple bottom.

You might quibble with pattern B, and this is certainly a hard triple bottom to find. Cover up the additional valleys after the right one and it looks like a

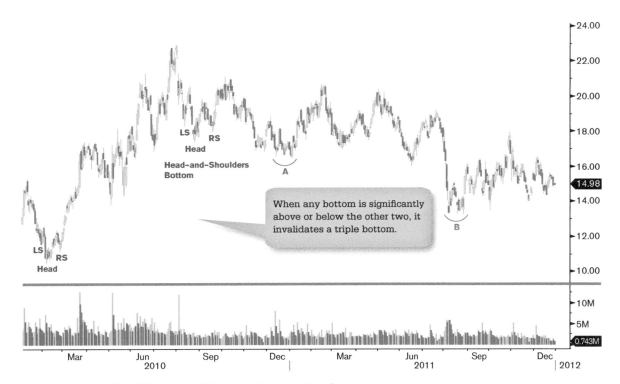

Exhibit 13.7: TIE US Equity (Titanium Metals Corp)

triple bottom. Price confirms this, too, by closing above the highest peak between the three valleys. Once the pattern confirms as a triple bottom, it does not matter if the stock nosedives into the ground or flies to the stars. The pattern remains a valid triple bottom.

Triple bottom C is a small one that you may have overlooked. It is valid, too.

The head-and-shoulders is a three valley pattern, but the head is well below the surrounding shoulders. It is not a triple bottom.

In the next chapter, we abandon bottoms and switch to tops: double tops. I like my double tops shaken, not stirred.

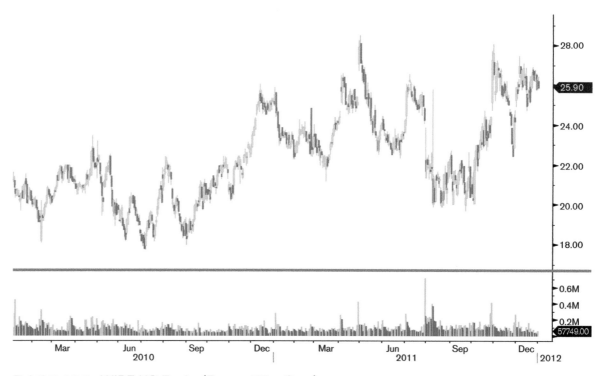

Exhibit 13.8: WIRE US Equity (Encore Wire Corp)

Exhibit 13.9: WIRE US Equity (Encore Wire Corp)

Test Yourself

Answer the following.

1. How many bottoms in a triple bottom need to be at exactly the same price?
   A. None
   B. One
   C. Two
   D. Three

2. True or false: If price does not close above the highest peak between the three bottoms, it is not a triple bottom.

3. True or false: If the middle bottom is well below the other two, the chart pattern could be a head-and-shoulders bottom.

4. In a triple bottom, price should bottom near the same price. What does "near" mean?
   A. Within 25 cents of each other.
   B. It depends on the price scale.
   C. It depends on the height of the triple bottom.
   D. It should *look* like they bottom near the same price.
   E. B and D.

Answers: 1. A; 2. True; 3. True; 4. E

Double Tops

Double tops are dual price mountains that peak near the same price. They are the same as double bottoms except flipped upside down. In this chapter, we will discuss what to look for when searching for double tops.

Exhibit 14.1 shows two examples of double tops on the daily scale. At F, price begins the steep march up the sides of the double top. It peaks at A, withdraws to G, and then forms another peak, B, at a price similar to A.

When price closes below G, it confirms the twin peaks as a valid double top.

I chose this chart because the long climb up reminds me of a trek up K2. The double top acts like storm clouds, warning of the coming decline.

Look at CDE. This is a triple top, but is CD also a double top? Yes. CD confirms as a double top before peak E forms. When E appears, the double top also becomes a triple top, but only when the trio confirms.

What do I mean by confirmation, and what should you look for in double tops? That question brings us to identification.

Identification Guidelines

The following table lists the criteria that double tops share.

Characteristic	Discussion
Upward price trend	The short-term price trend leading to the double top is up.
Two peaks	Look for two peaks that top out near the same price. Near means within about 3 percent. The tops should *look* as if they are at the same price.

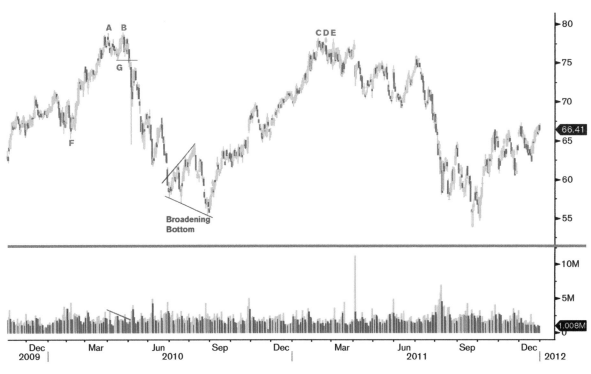

Exhibit 14.1: GD US Equity (General Dynamics Corp)

Characteristic	Discussion
Peak separation	The time between peaks varies, but two to six weeks is typical.
Valley	The valley drop between the two peaks should measure at least 10 percent, but allow exceptions. The drop should look proportional to the width of the double top.
Volume	Volume is usually higher on the left top than the right, but this is an observation, not a requirement.
Confirmation	Price must close below the lowest valley between the two peaks. If price closes above the highest peak before confirmation, it invalidates the double top.

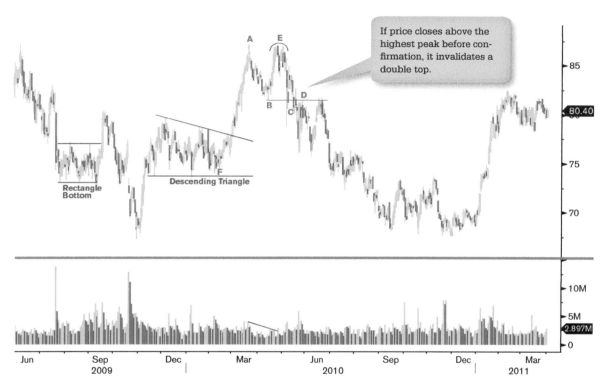

If price closes above the highest peak before confirmation, it invalidates a double top.

Exhibit 14.2: LMT US Equity (Lockheed Martin Corp)

Consider the double top shown in Exhibit 14.2.

Price begins the upward trend at F, leading to the double top. Twin peaks appear as an Adam & Eve double top at the cleverly chosen letters A and E. The double top begins to reverse the FA climb.

The time between the two peaks is usually less than two months, frequently ranging between two and six weeks. They can be further apart, especially when using the weekly or monthly scales, or narrower for day traders.

The valley between the two peaks sees price drop, but the depth should be proportional to the width of the peaks. Peaks separated by two weeks probably will not see a massive plunge between the two tops.

Usually the drop measures in the 10 to 20 percent range, but allow exceptions, especially when using other time scales (like intraday).

Volume tends to be higher on formation of the left peak than the right, which this example shows.

The twin peaks become a valid double top when price closes below the valley between the two peaks. The valley bottom is at B and it confirms at C when the red candle closes below the price of B. A pullback to the breakout price at D gives traders another opportunity to exit before the decline resumes.

Double Top Psychology

Why do double tops form? The answer is the same as it is for other chart patterns: fear and greed, sometimes powered by fundamentals.

Exhibit 14.3 shows an example of a double top standing like a castle overlooking a sea of prices.

At C, the company released first quarter earnings and announced the completion of a merger with Amrep Inc., a chemical supplier. The stock went nowhere that day.

Two days later, the institutions finished digesting the news and decided the stock represented a good value. Their buying pushed the stock up the price mountain to A where traders encountered a group of angry bears. The bears pushed them off the cliff, forcing the stock back down.

Since the bears remained at the top of the cliff, the bulls bought the stock at the bottom and their buying demand made it climb back up a new slope to B, forming a second peak.

A day later, a brokerage firm downgraded the stock.

The bulls and bears fought again, tearing into each other, but not making or losing much ground. Even so, the smart money started selling ahead of the second quarter's earnings announcement.

At E, the company reported earnings and had a conference call to discuss them the next day. The news herded some of the bulls into the slaughterhouse and bears pushed the rest over the edge. The stock did a cliff diver plunge back to the sea at D.

Variations

I show variations of the basic double top, beginning with Exhibit 14.4.

I have already discussed Adam and Eve double bottoms, and the top variety is similar to the bottoms. Adam peaks are narrow, often one-day price spikes. Eve peaks look more rounded. If she has price spikes, they are numerous and short.

The exhibit shows an Adam & Adam double top at AA. Following that, an Eve & Adam top appears. Notice how wide Eve appears compared to Adam. Another Eve & Adam double top appears about a year later.

Exhibit 14.5 shows the two missing varieties of Adam and Eve.

An Adam & Eve double top appears in February, and you may be scratching your head because the two

Exhibit 14.7: COH US Equity (Coach Inc)

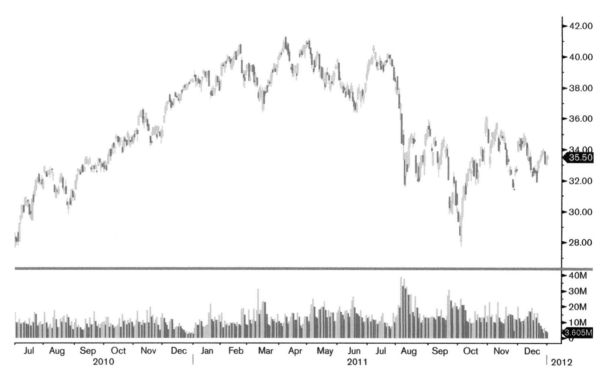

Exhibit 14.8: XLB US Equity (Materials Select Sector SPDR Fund)

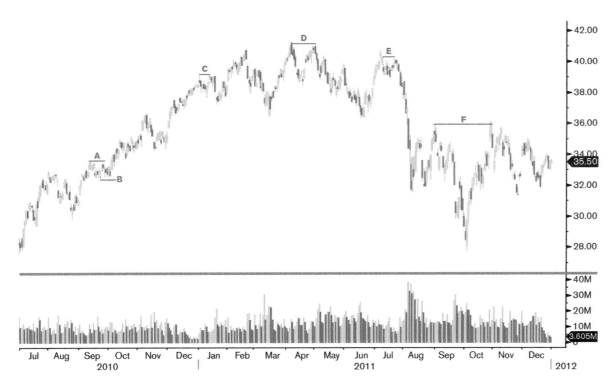

Exhibit 14.9: XLB US Equity (Materials Select Sector SPDR Fund)

Test Yourself

Answer the following.

1. True or false: A double top is composed of two peaks near the same price.

2. A double top has how many valleys between the two peaks?

   A. 1

   B. 2

   C. 3

   D. At least 1

3. True or false: An unconfirmed twin peak pattern is not a double top.

Answers: 1. True; 2. D; 3. True

CHAPTER 15

Triple Tops

A double top can become a triple after growing another peak near the same price. Let us take a closer look at this medical miracle to see how traders recognize it.

Exhibit 15.1 shows two examples of real triple tops and one implant.

The triple top at A has three peaks near the same price after the stock trends upward into the chart pattern. The stock becomes a base jumper and confirms the chart pattern on the way down through the horizontal red line.

The middle triple top, at B, is also a triple top with the same features as A. The skydiver pops his chute, and the drop ends soon after.

C is not a triple top because it does not confirm. You can guess what that means, but the next section makes the various components of a triple top clear.

Identification Guidelines

The following table lists guidelines for finding triple tops.

Characteristic	Discussion
Upward price trend	The short-term price trend leading to the triple top is up.
Three peaks	Look for three minor highs. Sometimes the peaks can be one-day price spikes or wider, more rounded turns. Each peak tends to look similar to the others, but allow variations.
Same price	Each minor high should peak *near* the same price. Rarely will all three top out at exactly the same price, so be flexible. In fact, the middle peak is sometimes lower than the other two.

> **KEY POINT:**
>
> A triple top is a three-peak pattern with the three minor highs topping out near the same price. The pattern acts as a reversal of the upward price trend.

Exhibit 15.1: ALK US Equity (Alaska Air Group Inc)

Characteristic	Discussion
Volume	Volume recedes, meaning it is higher on the left than the right, but each peak can show significant volume. Do not exclude a pattern because it has an unusual volume shape.
Confirmation	Price must confirm the triple top by closing below the lowest valley between the three peaks.

Exhibit 15.2 shows another example of a triple top. I chose this one because the middle peak is depressed and needed cheering up. Do not trash a valid triple top because the middle peak is slightly lower than its neighbors.

Price trends upward from below the chart pattern at E. Peaks A and C have more rounded looking turns than does needle B, but that is fine.

To confirm a triple top, price has to close below the lowest valley in the chart pattern. That happens at D.

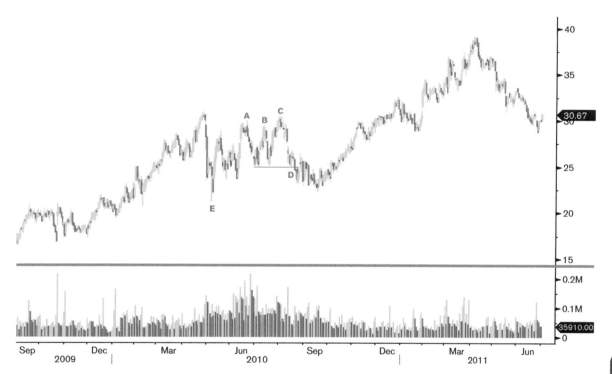

Exhibit 15.2: SXI US Equity (Standex International Corp)

Volume trends downward as the blue line shows. Receding volume is typical of triple tops, but do not discard a potential triple top because of unusual volume.

Triple Top Psychology

Exhibit 15.3 shows selling near a fixed price that halts the upward movement in the stock, forming triple top ABC. It might play out something like this.

Imagine that you run a hedge fund that bought the stock at 18 in 2009 just after the bear market ended (not shown). At A, the stock reached 38 and change, more than double what you paid. Based on your analysis, it is time to sell.

However, since you own a large position, you cannot just dump your shares on the market all at once. That would force the stock down into the Hudson faster than an airliner striking a flock of birds.

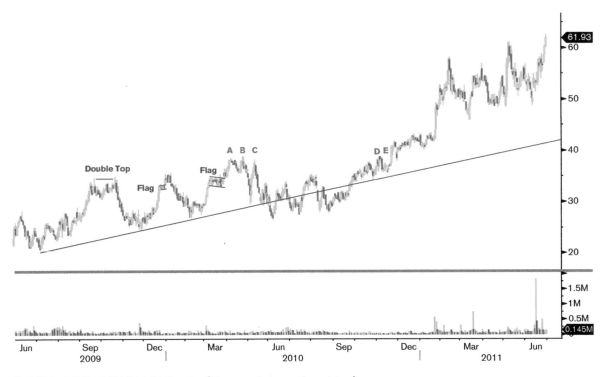

Exhibit 15.3: HAYN US Equity (Haynes International Inc)

At A, you let loose your first volley, but since the stock is thinly traded (less than 40,000 shares), you have difficulty selling 10,000 share blocks. You have to break it up into smaller chunks each day.

At B, you are having a bad day. You feel frustrated because other trades are going badly and you need to raise cash to cover redemptions. Your selling punishes the stock. Others see the panic selling and join in, sending the stock tumbling below 30.

At C, the stock is once again at your sell price, but you still have plenty of this lame turkey left in your portfolio. You sell as quietly as you can, as quickly as you can, but others sense the weakness and sell, too. Together, that sends the stock plunging quicker than a submarine during a crash dive. Momentum grows, keeping the stock trending down.

The stock reaches a long-term trendline (shown in blue) and bobbles up and down along that line for months. When the stock recovers to D, you sell more shares and finish dumping them when the stock powers higher at E.

Now that you have sold your position, the stock doubles, which really pisses you off.

Variations

Only one variation needs to concern you: a head-and-shoulders top. In the next two chapters, we discuss head-and-shoulders patterns but until then, just avoid picking triple tops in which the center peak rises too far above the other two. It should not look like a person's bust.

For example, consider Exhibit 15.4.

The head-and-shoulders has a head above the shoulders (LS and RS) far enough to make it look like a person's bust.

Compare that to the triple top ABC. B is slightly above A and C, but hardly enough to notice. It *looks* like a triple top and not a head-and-shoulders top.

Exercise

The first exercise is easy (see Exhibit 15.5). Find at least one triple top, a head-and-shoulders top (guess), and a double top. Except for the head-and-shoulders top, you should be able to identify the other patterns.

When searching for a triple top, imagine the outline of a mountain range. Three of the mountains line up at the same height to form a triple top.

Exhibit 15.6 shows the answers.

The head-and-shoulders top has a head sticking above the other two peaks, helping to differentiate it from a triple top.

The triple top at ABC forms three peaks near the same price. It confirms when price closes below the lowest valley in the chart pattern.

The double top may have given you some trouble because the two peaks are not at the same price (45 cents difference, or less than 1 percent).

Peak D is not a triple top. I shy away from peaks that align like this one does, forming a diagonal trend downward. Often that is a clue to a symmetrical triangle.

Exhibit 15.7 shows a target-rich environment. In it you should find at least two triple tops, two flags, a pennant, a double bottom, and a head-and-shoulders top.

Exhibit 15.8 shows where the chart patterns are located. Starting on the left, a small head-and-shoulders top appears in April. Since the price difference between the first two peaks is just 15 cents, if you want to call this a triple top, fine.

Next is the large pattern ABC. Although these three peaks line up near the same price, the chart pattern does not confirm, so it is not a triple top.

The flag in July is difficult to spot because it acts as a reversal of the uptrend.

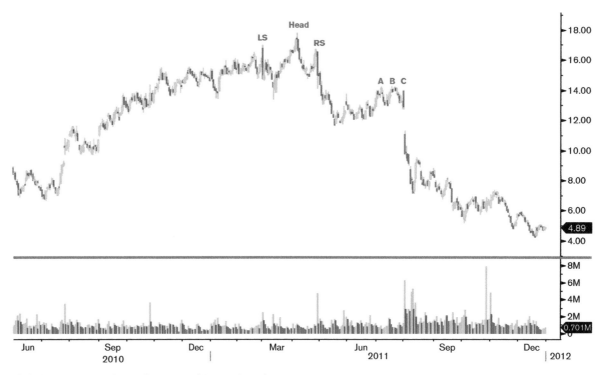

Exhibit 15.4: FOE US Equity (Ferro Corp)

The December flag and February pennant follow price higher surrounding the holidays.

D is the first triple top. The upward spike that occurs after the third peak also occurs after confirmation. The chart pattern reversal leads to a huge drop that sees a double bottom form as another reversal.

Following that is the second triple top, at E.

In the next chapter, I discuss head-and-shoulders bottoms. Just two days ago, I received an e-mail asking why I have not discussed the inverted head-and-shoulders pattern. I do not call them by that name. It has something to do with the federal eyewitness protection program.

Test Yourself

Answer the following.

1. If a fourth peak appears at the same price as the other three, what does it mean?
   A. If price closes below the lowest valley in the triple top before the fourth peak appears, you have a valid triple top.
   B. If the triple top is unconfirmed, it becomes a quad or multiple top pattern.
   C. If the four-peak pattern confirms, it suggests price is going down.
   D. Overhead resistance is strong.
   E. All of the above.

2. True or false: If price trends lower into a three-peak pattern, you have a triple top.

3. How close do the peaks have to be from each other to qualify as a triple top?
   A. It depends on scaling.
   B. No more than 25 cents.
   C. Within 4 percent.
   D. It does not matter providing they appear near the same price.
   E. All of the above.

4. True or false: Triple tops tend to be wide patterns with many lasting from two to three months.

Answers: 1. E; 2. False; 3. A or D; 4. True

CHAPTER 16

Head-and-Shoulders Bottoms

The head-and-shoulders is perhaps the best-known chart pattern. It has an evocative name, but recognizing a valid one takes an understanding of the rules. Let us begin by looking at a few samples. (See Exhibit 16.1.)

In this exhibit, I show three head-and-shoulders patterns. Pattern A is a head-and-shoulders bottom. The right shoulder (RS) bottoms at a price above the left (LS), but not too far. If this were the bust of a real person, yes, they might be in need of medical attention.

Notice that the head is below the adjacent shoulders. That is a key feature of a head-and-shoulders bottom.

Pattern B is similar to A. The two shoulders bottom close to the same price and they are almost symmetrical about the head in terms of time. Symmetry is important to head-and-shoulders patterns.

C is a good example of a head-and-shoulders top. That chart pattern is the subject of the next chapter.

Besides a miracle, what does it take to find a valid head-and-shoulders bottom?

Identification Guidelines

The following table lists the identification guidelines.

Characteristic	Discussion
Downward price trend	Look for a short-term price trend leading down to the head-and-shoulders bottom.
Three valleys	The head-and-shoulders is a three valley pattern with the middle valley bottoming below the other two. The three valleys and two armpits (peaks between the valleys) should be well-defined minor highs and lows.

KEY POINT:

A head-and-shoulders bottom is a three-valley chart pattern that resembles a person's bust, inverted. The head is below the adjacent shoulders, and it acts as a reversal of the downward price trend.

Characteristic	Discussion
Symmetry	The entire pattern has a symmetrical feel to it. The left and right shoulders should have similar distances to the head; both should bottom at or near the same price, and be positioned on either side of the head.
Volume	Weakest on the right shoulder and often highest on the left shoulder, but head volume can be high, too. Do not exclude a head-and-shoulders bottom because of an unusual volume pattern.
Neckline, confirmation	The neckline is a line drawn across the two armpits. A close above this line confirms the head-and-shoulders as a valid chart pattern. For up-sloping necklines, use a close above the right armpit as the confirmation price.

Exhibit 16.2 shows one valid head-and-shoulders bottom and a wannabe. Let us determine the differences.

Pattern AB is a valid head-and-shoulders bottom. From the peak in February, price tumbles down a waterfall into the chart pattern and forms the left shoulder as a minor low. Following that, a lower valley appears as the head. After recovering from the head, price makes a higher low that becomes the right shoulder.

Points A and B are the armpits. Connecting those is the neckline, shown in red.

The two shoulders are almost the same distance from the head, but hardly bottom at the same price. It is hard to tell which of the three valleys have higher volume.

In other words, the guidelines are just that, guidelines, not firm rules. Be flexible when prospecting for head-and-shoulders bottoms since wide variations are common.

Pattern DEF would seem to be a better example of a head-and-shoulders bottom. The two shoulders are more symmetrical looking both in price level and head distance. The pattern confirms when price closes above the neckline.

What is the flaw? Answer: The left shoulder is not a valid minor low. Recall that a minor low should be the lowest price from five days before to five days after. The left shoulder appears to be just a small blip in a rising price trend and not a minor low.

Head-and-Shoulders Bottom Psychology

Why do head-and-shoulders bottoms form? The chart pattern represents the struggle to find the lowest price at the best value. (See Exhibit 16.3.)

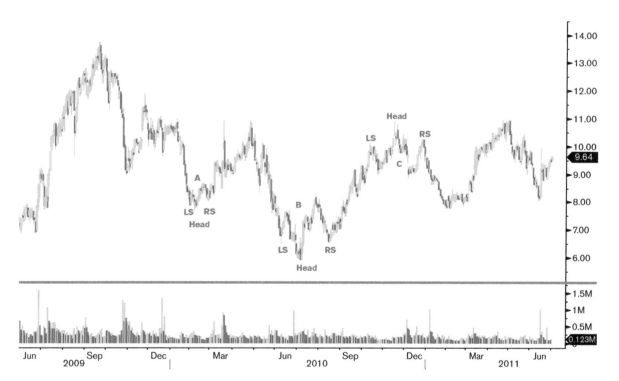

Exhibit 16.1: SMRT US Equity (Stein Mart Inc)

For example, the chart shows volume spiking even as the stock descends, going into the left shoulder. That higher turnover is a sign of a bottom, but one the stock has seen plenty of times as it rolled down the hill from the January high. What is different this time?

Buying demand puts a crimp on the downward slide and price moves up, but only for about a week. Then, the downtrend resumes, going into the head. Volume on formation of the head is less than on the left shoulder, but that configuration is typical for head-and-shoulders bottoms.

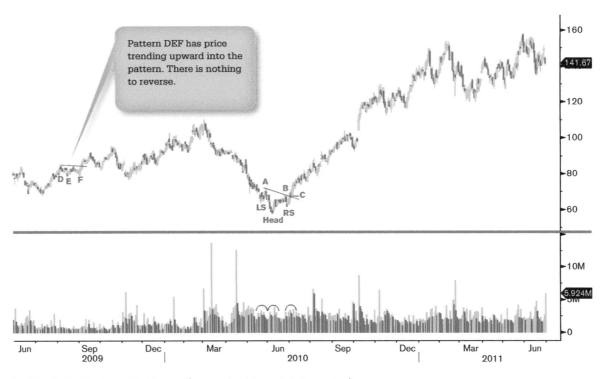

Exhibit 16.2: CF US Equity (CF Industries Holdings Inc)

The smart money is accumulating the stock in anticipation of a change in the fundamentals and a rising price. The stock finds support and bottoms at the head low. Then the stock begins recovering, taking volume with it, signaling the change from bear to bull.

Price rounds over at the right armpit and drops to form the right shoulder. Volume is subdued here as if the smart money knows a good value when they see it, but are keeping it quiet. Their buying sends the stock moving higher again, above the neckline, confirming the turn from bear to bull.

Now firmly entrenched in their positions, the smart money can sip margaritas while others do the hard work of pushing the stock higher.

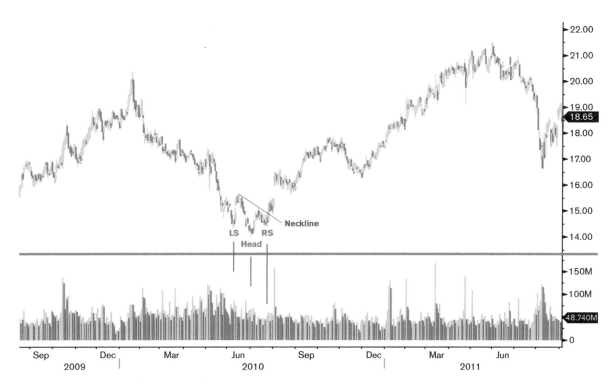

Exhibit 16.3: PFE US Equity (Pfizer Inc)

Variations

I show Exhibit 16.4 because of the right head-and-shoulders bottom (the one with measles). What is so special about this one compared to the others? It has multiple shoulders.

The right shoulder has two small valleys and the left has three. I show four of them as red dots. Strictly speaking, only two of these five are minor lows because of the five-day count on either side of the low to qualify it as a minor low.

This variation is called a complex head-and-shoulders bottom. Those are chart patterns with multiple shoulders, multiple heads, or both (rarely). As you scan for head-and-shoulders bottoms, look to the left and

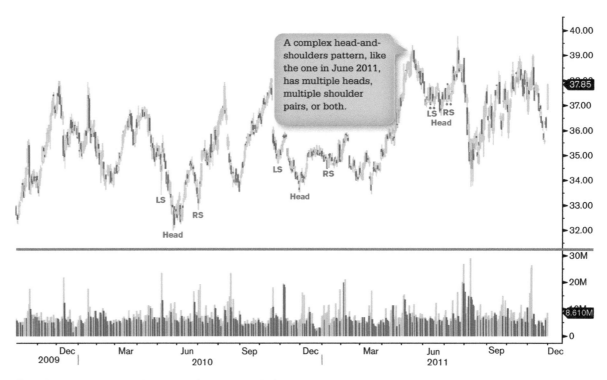

A complex head-and-shoulders pattern, like the one in June 2011, has multiple heads, multiple shoulder pairs, or both.

Exhibit 16.4: LLY US Equity (Eli Lilly & Co)

right and check for additional shoulders or another head. Treat the more complex pattern as a simple head-and-shoulders bottom.

As for the other two head-and-shoulders bottoms, notice the higher left shoulder bottom in each case. Irregularities such as these will cause doubt until you become accustomed to identifying flawed patterns.

Exhibit 16.5 shows a chart pattern that you may think is a head-and-shoulders bottom, and you would be wrong. This one has two twists. What are they?

First, price does not trend downward into the chart pattern as the blue channel lines show. Price rises instead. This head-and-shoulders acts as a continuation of the upward price trend and not a reversal.

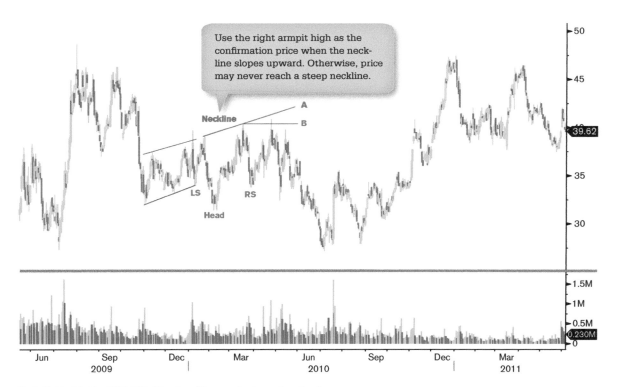

Use the right armpit high as the confirmation price when the neckline slopes upward. Otherwise, price may never reach a steep neckline.

Exhibit 16.5: TXI US Equity (Texas Industries Inc)

One might argue that point, saying that price drops from the peak in July 2009 and bottoms a year later with the middle section being a retrace of that downtrend. Fine.

The second "flaw" is that it never confirms as a valid head-and-shoulders bottom. That means price did not *close* above the neckline (A) or right armpit high (B) before closing below the bottom of the pattern. The armpit measure is the correct one to use when the neckline slopes upward, as in this case.

Exercise

The first exercise shows three head-and-shoulders bottoms, but one you may disagree with. See if you can find all three. (See Exhibit 16.6.)

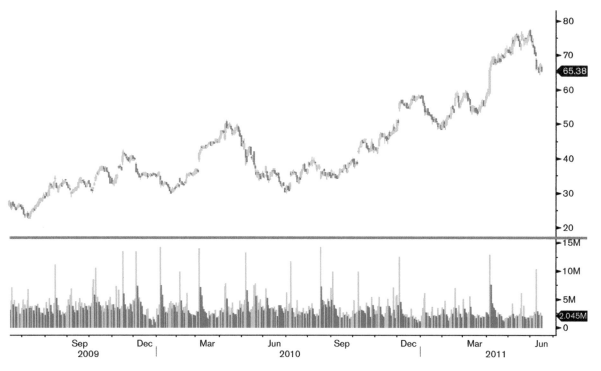

Exhibit 16.6: ANF US Equity (Abercrombie & Fitch Co)

Exhibit 16.7 shows the answers. The questionable head-and-shoulders bottom is at A. Why? Because price trends upward into the chart pattern. It does not act as a "bottom" reversal but as a continuation pattern.

The other two chart patterns are valid head-and-shoulders bottoms. They reverse the short-term downtrend.

Note the horizontal red confirmation line in patterns A and B where the neckline slopes upward.

The next exercise is easier, but just as tricky. There is at least one head-and-shoulders bottom in Exhibit 16.8. See how many you can find.

Exhibit 16.9 shows the answers. Pattern A is not a head-and-shoulders bottom. Why? Because it is not

CHAPTER 17

Head-and-Shoulders Tops

Spotting tops is easier for me. Perhaps it is the idea that preservation of capital is more important than profit. Whatever the reason, let us look at the last chart pattern in this section of the book.

The head-and-shoulders top appears on the chart just as it sounds and Exhibit 17.1 shows examples. In both chart patterns, a head towers above the shoulders, making it look like a person's bust.

Price trends upward into the head-and-shoulders reversal. Then a left shoulder forms (LS), followed by a head and right shoulder. When price closes below the neckline, it confirms the chart pattern as valid. Price drops like a falling climber whose pitons have released.

Identification Guidelines

The following table lists guidelines for identifying head-and-shoulders tops.

Characteristic	Discussion
Upward price trend	Look for an upward price trend leading to a head-and-shoulders top.
Three peaks	The head-and-shoulders top is a three-peak pattern with the middle peak above the other two. The three peaks and two armpits (valleys between the peaks) should be well-defined minor highs and lows.
Symmetry	The entire pattern has a symmetrical feel to it. The left and right shoulders should have similar distances from the head; both shoulders should top out near the same price, and be positioned on either side of the head.

KEY POINT:

A head-and-shoulders top is a three-peak reversal pattern with a centrally located head priced above two adjacent (shoulder) peaks. The pattern confirms as a valid chart pattern when price closes below the neckline or right armpit.

Characteristic	Discussion
Volume	Weakest on the right shoulder and often highest on the left shoulder, but head volume can be high, too. Do not exclude a head-and-shoulders top because of an unusual volume pattern.
Neckline, confirmation	The neckline is a line drawn across the two armpits. A close below this line confirms the head-and-shoulders as a valid chart pattern. For down-sloping necklines, use a close below the right armpit as the confirmation price.

Exhibit 17.2 shows a head-and-shoulders top on the weekly scale. It appears as a three-bump pattern sitting atop a hill as if it were playing King of the Mountain.

Notice that the chart pattern on the weekly scale appears similar to ones on the daily chart or any other scale.

Two shoulders appear at similar distances from the head, but not quite at the same price, with a head that towers above the shoulders.

This head-and-shoulders top has a down-sloping neckline in red (A). The blue line (B) shows how much sooner price validates the pattern when using a close below the right armpit instead of the neckline.

Volume is higher on the left shoulder than the right.

Head-and-Shoulders Top Psychology

Why do head-and-shoulders tops form? Pretend that you represent the smart money—high wealth individuals, financial institutions, hedge or mutual funds. You are searching for a stock to buy and believe that Hovnanian, shown in Exhibit 17.3, represents an intriguing situation.

You start buying at A, and that buying pressure sends the stock exploding out of a loose consolidation region that ended in March.

Others join in and buy the stock, sending the price into orbit like a shuttle launching.

As stars appear out the shuttle's window and the stock rises above 7, you have made 40 percent in about two weeks. Time to sell.

Your selling causes the stock to halt its upward move and begin a retrace, forming the left shoulder.

Sensing weakness, you stop selling but monitor the situation. Buy-the-dip players, believing that this is a chance to get in on a mission to deep space, buy the stock on the retrace. The decline halts, and the stock begins rising again.

As the stock moves up, momentum players join the trend. Once the stock rises above 8, you resume selling, not heavily at first because you have a large number of shares to dump. Still, the market players notice your selling and the stock heads back down.

You dump your remaining shares as the stock begins tumbling. Volume rises as other players sell their

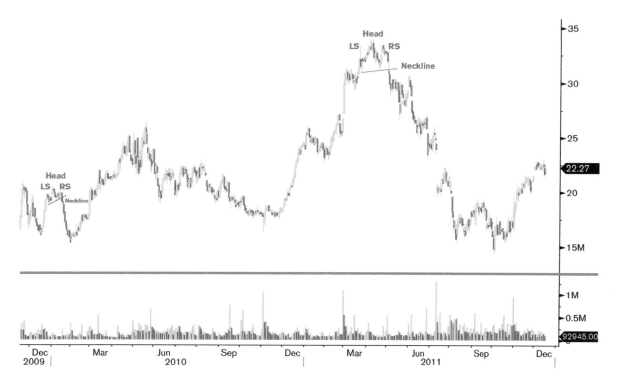

Exhibit 17.1: TREX US Equity (Trex Co Inc)

shares to unsuspecting buyers. The stock continues moving down and slides back below 6. Believing the stock oversold, demand picks up and sends the price moving up again for the last time.

You watch from the sidelines. The stock climbs to form the right shoulder. Lacking support for a continued rise, the stock turns down.

Investors versed in technical analysis see the head-and-shoulders top for what it is: a reversal. They quietly take profits. Others initiate short sales by selling high and hoping price hits zero.

The stock moves lower and forms a pennant before breaking out downward, leading to a head-and-shoulders bottom reversal.

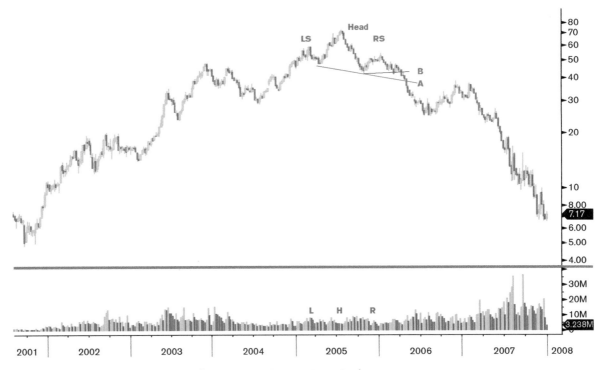

Exhibit 17.2: HOV US Equity (Hovnanian Enterprises Inc)

Variations

Exhibit 17.4 shows a variety of head-and-shoulders tops. Let us begin on the left.

The head-and-shoulders at A is a traditional-looking pattern because it has wide, rounded shoulders and deep recessions that form the armpits. The pattern confirms when price closes below the horizontal line.

Pattern B is an outlier. The left and right shoulders do not qualify as minor highs because they are not wide enough, and yet the head-and-shoulders acts

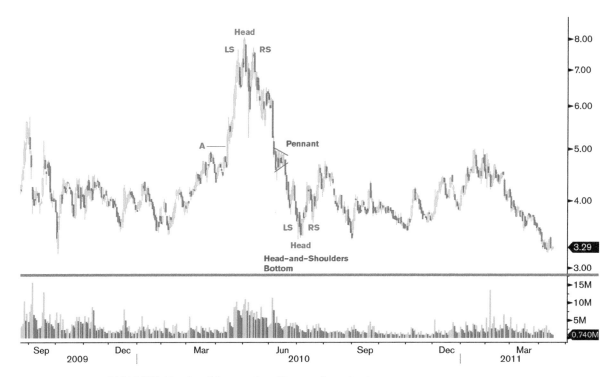

Exhibit 17.3: HOV US Equity (Hovnanian Enterprises Inc)

as a reversal of the uptrend. It confirms when price closes below the up-sloping neckline.

Pattern C has a spike for its head with unevenly priced shoulders, but they are close to symmetrical about the head. The pattern also confirms when price closes below the up-sloping neckline.

Pattern D is the only invalid head-and-shoulders top. The left shoulder is much wider than the right one, and the two shoulders are not symmetrical about the head.

Notice that the stock closes above the top of the head (E) before price closes below the red confirmation line, invalidating the chart pattern.

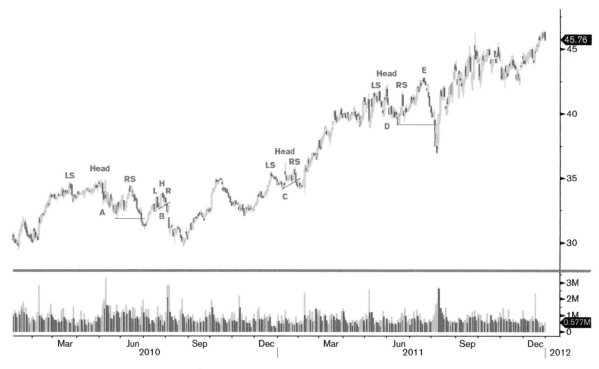

Exhibit 17.4: CHD US Equity (Church & Dwight Co Inc)

When searching for head-and-shoulders tops, I have found it beneficial to ask if the pattern *looks* like a person's bust. If the neck is unusually long or if the two shoulders are crooked, then look for another head-and-shoulders top.

Exercise

In this exercise, find as many head-and-shoulders tops as you can. Also, look for double and triple tops and bottoms, ascending and descending triangles. (See Exhibit 17.5.)

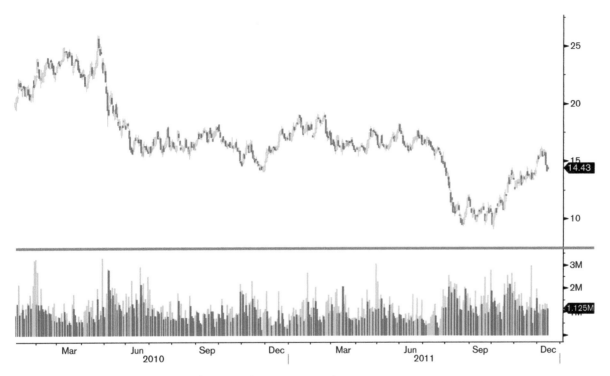

Exhibit 17.5: RYL US Equity (Ryland Group Inc/The)

The answers appear in Exhibit 17.6. I show the patterns spread out like peanut butter across bread, but there are other patterns that may qualify (like additional double bottoms or double tops).

Head-and-shoulders tops A, B, and C are all valid. Pattern D confirms as a head-and-shoulders top, but the trend is downward leading to the chart pattern. It is not a reversal, but a continuation head-and-shoulders top.

Notice that since the head-and-shoulders pattern appeared at the end of the trend, the downward breakout did not amount to much. That is a trading tip you might want to remember.

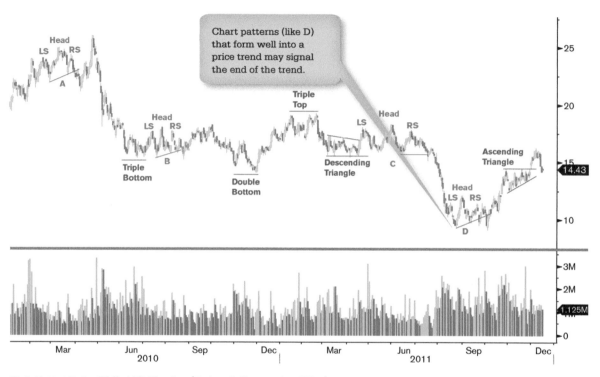

Exhibit 17.6: RYL US Equity (Ryland Group Inc/The)

As for the other chart patterns, the double bottom in November 2010 has uneven bottoms (3 percent apart), making the pattern difficult to identify.

Exhibit 17.7 has many patterns that look like head-and-shoulders tops, but are not. Find two valid ones.

Exhibit 17.8 shows the answers. The valid head-and-shoulders tops are marked A and B, flavored with red necklines. The other chart patterns do not confirm before price rises above the top of the chart pattern.

The video Necklines and Breakouts has nothing to do with acne. Rather, it shows how to use necklines to determine the breakout from head-and-shoulders tops and bottoms.

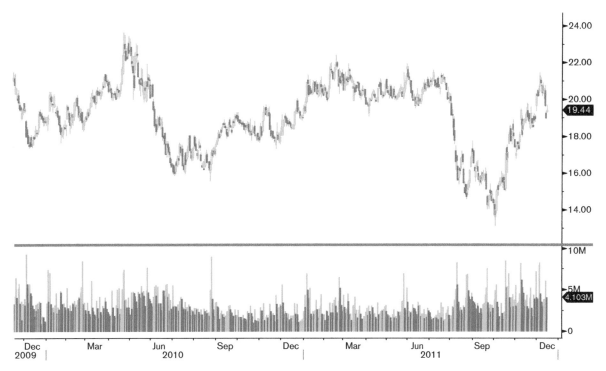

Exhibit 17.7: TOL US Equity (Toll Brothers Inc)

Video:
Necklines and Breakouts

www.wiley.com/go/bulkowskivg/Video3

It's a Wrap

This chapter completes the introduction to chart pattern identification. We learned to use horizontal trendlines to highlight rectangles. Then we sloped one of the lines to find ascending and descending

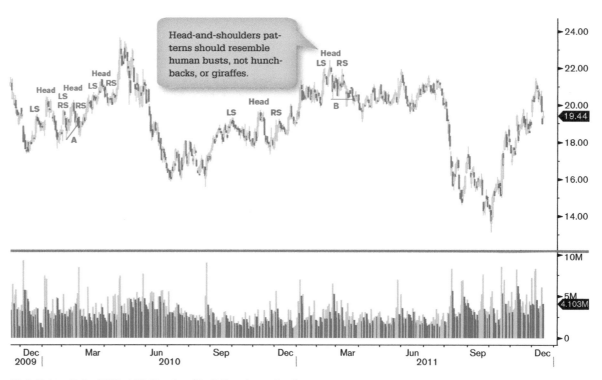

Exhibit 17.8: TOL US Equity (Toll Brothers Inc)

triangles. Two converging trendlines outlined a symmetrical triangle.

After that, we switched to peaks and valleys to find double and triple tops and bottoms. Completing the group were the head-and-shoulders, a complex pattern that is not much different from a triple top or bottom.

Now that we know what to look for, we can use the patterns as buy signals. The next section describes how.

CHAPTER 18

Basic Buy Setups

This chapter begins looking at chart patterns as trading tools. Now that we can identify chart patterns, we can use these tools as signals to help time our entry into the markets.

The basic setup rules are the same for most of the chart patterns we have covered. Here they are.

Setup Rules:

1. Place a buy stop a penny above the top trendline to catch the upward breakout.
2. Once into the trade, place a stop a penny below the bottom of the chart pattern.

Notice the absence of moving averages and other indicators. Simple is best.

I tested this setup on most of the chart patterns in this book and discuss those results later. Here are actual trades I made that show how the signals work.

Ascending Triangle Buy Signal

When price breaks out upward from an ascending triangle, buy. For example, pictured in Exhibit 18.1 is a trade I made in one.

In my trading notebook, I wrote, "Oils are hot, and I think this stock has room to grow. Plus, it pays a dividend. Book score is –1, but that expects a throwback, and I'll be happy if price comes close to the predicted 65.91 book score target."

The book score I mention is from my *Trading Classic Chart Patterns* book, which discusses a scoring system to rate the probability of price reaching a target. In this case, the target was 65.91, and the system suggested that it would be difficult for the stock to climb that far before tumbling. It was right.

The day before the breakout, I placed a buy stop at 52.06, which is a penny above the top of the triangle. It filled the next day at 52.07, A.

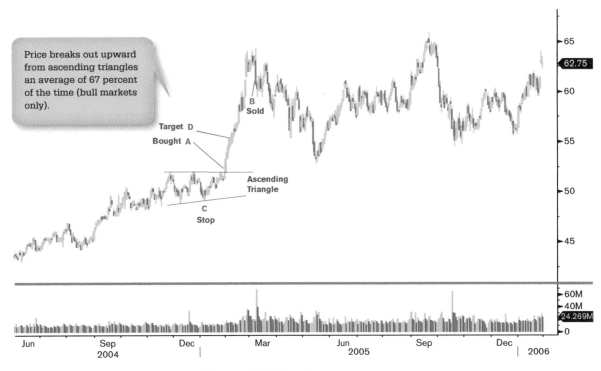

Exhibit 18.1: XOM US Equity (Exxon Mobil Corp)

Placing a buy order a penny *above* the top trendline is important since additional peaks may stop right at the line.

I placed a stop below the minor low at C, 49.21. If the chart pattern is tall, a stop located below the bottom of the chart pattern can entail a significant loss. Instead, I located the stop closer.

I used the measure rule, which I will discuss in Chapter 24, to calculate a price target and came up with 55.20. I show that on the chart as D. As the chart shows, the stock pretended it was an untethered helium balloon and soared.

Although I do not show them, I raised the stop seven times as price climbed. The highest stop was at 61.15 and it filled at 60.90, B, in a late-day sell-off that popped the balloon and blew through my stop on the way down.

I made 17 percent on this trade in 37 days.

Exhibit 18.2: BRC US Equity (Brady Corp)

Descending Triangle Buy Signal

A descending triangle with an upward breakout is one of my favorite chart patterns to trade, and Exhibit 18.2 shows how I do it.

On May 16, the company announced earnings and scheduled a conference call the next morning to discuss it. I vowed to buy the stock if it gapped open higher. That is what happened.

However, I will not chase a stock. When I looked at it after the open, it had climbed to 34 from the prior day's close at 33.46, so I took half of that and placed a limit order to buy at 33.78. That filled.

The bottom of the triangle was at 32.50, so I placed a stop at 32.46, below the minor low at C. The upside target was 34.50, set up by overhead resistance at A (circled) and a taller band above that, starting at 36 (D). Those two prices were not true sell targets, but locations where the stock might plow into difficulty. They would become sell points if I thought price was going to reverse.

Price climbed for several days, but my notes warned of (1) candles getting shorter, (2) price stalling at the gap (E), (3) completion of a Big W pattern (AB), and (4) price exceeding my original target. The possibility of continued gains decreased, so I decided to sell and received an average price of about 36.80. I made 9 percent in 6 days.

Symmetrical Triangle Buy Signal

Symmetrical triangles tend to be prolific chart patterns and that means plenty of trading opportunities. Here is a long-term trade I made using a large triangle. (See Exhibit 18.3.)

I watched the stock for a few months before buying at the open the day after it broke out upward (A). This purchase used a combination of good fundamentals and the symmetrical triangle. I received a fill at 28 with a target of 56. Since it was a long-term holding, I did not use an initial stop loss order. However, in late April, I started using a stop and raised it four times.

On July 9, the stock looked like it was making a head-and-shoulders top. That scared me out of the position, so I sold it for a 30 percent profit, at 35.73 including four dividend payments.

The head-and-shoulders never confirmed, so it was a mistake selling. The stock climbed to 41.87 in October before dropping seven points in two days. Maybe selling was a good choice after all.

Double Bottom Buy Signal

The basic double bottom setup uses a buy stop a penny above the top of the chart pattern to get you into the trade in a timely matter. I do not recommend trading unconfirmed double bottoms. (See Exhibit 18.4.)

Double bottom AB appears on the weekly chart so I could show you the entire trade. I bought at the open the day after the double bottom confirmed and received a fill of 5.94 (C).

This double bottom has a tall left side, so I also called it a Big W chart pattern. The uneven bottoms (A and B) did not bother me.

In June 2009, one firm rated the stock a strong buy. Another said it was a strong sell. Go figure. One of them was wrong.

A year later, in early July 2010, I was getting worried. The stock had pierced trendline E (shown in blue). I was also predicting a bear market then. I started placing a stop and raising it as price climbed. However, about a week later, Intel said that they had the best quarter in a decade, so I figured this stock would do well, too. I canceled the stop.

In January 2011, I wrote in my notebook, "This looks like it's going to drop back to 13 then 12 then 11."

On February 16, I placed a stop below a minor low at 17.55 and the stock hit it a week later.

Exhibit 18.3: AIZ US Equity (Assurant Inc)

I made 194 percent during a hold time of 1 year and 10 months.

Head-and-Shoulders Bottom Buy Signal

The setup for head-and-shoulders is a bit different from the other chart patterns, so let us discuss it.

What are the trading rules for this setup?

1. A head-and-shoulders bottom appears on the price chart.
2. Place a buy stop a penny above the right armpit when the neckline slopes upward, or enter the day after price closes above a down-sloping neckline.
3. Once into the trade, place a stop loss order a penny below the head.

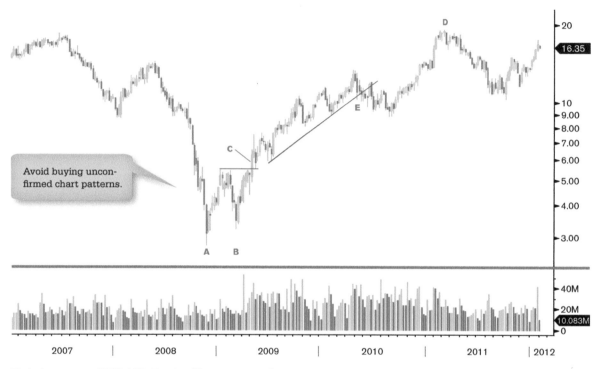

Avoid buying uncon-firmed chart patterns.

Exhibit 18.4: TER US Equity (Teradyne Inc)

Placing a stop a penny below the head means the trade will be stopped out 16 percent of the time, on average. To flip that around, the *most* you will win is 84 percent of the time, on average.

That is the theory, but how does it work in real life? Consider the trade I made shown in Exhibit 18.5.

A small head-and-shoulders bottom appears in January. The neckline is the blue line at B. When price closes above this line, since it slopes downward, it confirms the chart pattern. If the neckline sloped upward, then we would use the high price at the right armpit as the confirmation price.

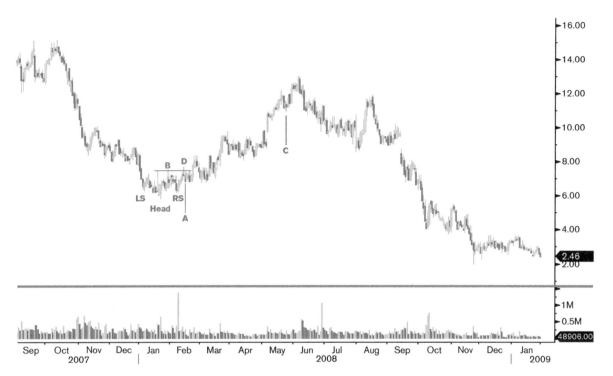

Exhibit 18.5: HHGP US Equity (Hudson Highland Group Inc)

I measured the rise from the right shoulder low to the peak at D and took 38 percent of that down from D as a limit price to buy the stock. The 38 percent is a Fibonacci number used to calculate how far price might retrace. The order filled at 7.06, at A.

Once into the trade, I placed a stop at 6.05, a dime below the right shoulder low.

I looked at the industry and found eight stocks that had hit bottom and were turning upward and four that were continuing lower.

The nice solid block of congestion immediately to the left of the right shoulder appealed to me (meaning underlying support). Since the general market was weak, I expected a throwback.

Although my notes do not say this, my guess is I probably drew the neckline to slice through the right armpit and rest on top of that consolidation area just below the letter B. That would mean a confirmed head-and-shoulders bottom.

I also made note of lots of insider buying during the month.

As price climbed, I raised the stop 13 times, resting at 11.03. Here is what I wrote about the sale. "Sell reason: My stop hit, just as I expected even though price closed higher. I tightened the stop because of the big 5+ percent decline yesterday for unexplained reasons (the market was also down big)."

The stock filled at 11.00 for a gain of 55 percent in about three months.

Rectangle Buy Signal

The trade I wanted to share was merged out of existence, so I have no chart. Instead, here are the rules to the traditional setup for trading rectangles.

1. Find a rectangle.
2. Place a buy order a penny above the top of the chart pattern.
3. If the order fills, place a stop a penny below the bottom of the chart pattern.

Exhibit 18.6 shows two rectangles with upward breakouts.

The first one breaks out at A, coasts upward to B, and then gets hammered, slowly. The stock bottoms

at C, conveniently stopping out traders that placed their stop just below the rectangle.

The rectangle at D fared better. Price broke out at D and made a determined climb to the summit at E. Thereafter, price formed a double top and that signaled an exit when price closed below the blue line, at G.

Notice the dip after the last touch, at H. Price touched the top trendline and dropped, but did not come close to the bottom trendline before reversing and staging an upward breakout.

That dip is what I call a partial decline. You must have a valid rectangle already in place (meaning at least two touches of each trendline, preferably three) before looking for a partial decline. A partial decline correctly predicts an immediate upward breakout 89 percent of the time according to two studies I did using 69 rectangle bottoms and another with 170 rectangle tops.

Triple Bottom Buy Signal

The following triple bottom trade is one in which I got lucky. (See Exhibit 18.7.)

I took a position in the stock on the basis of the triple bottom. However, notice that I bought before confirmation. Strictly speaking, that is a no-no. Oddly, I felt that the triple bottom would *not* confirm and I would be stopped out for a loss. But that did not stop me from going ahead with the trade anyway.

I received a fill at A, 10.78. I placed a stop at 9.89, which is below the minor low at C. I set my sights on

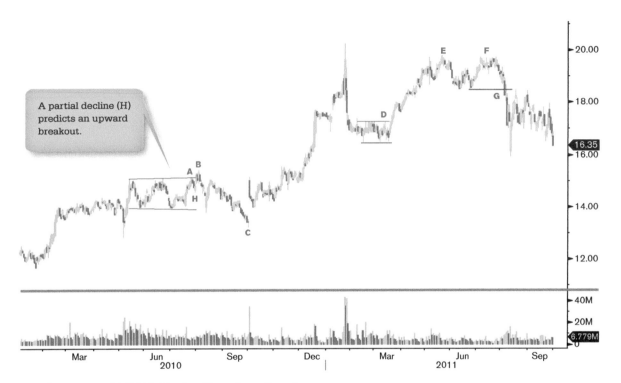

A partial decline (H) predicts an upward breakout.

Exhibit 18.6: SLE US Equity (Sara Lee Corp)

14, where the stock peaked in December 2004 and also the source of a long-term down-sloping trendline that connected the January 2004 high (not shown).

Over the weekend, I raised the stop to 10.17 and when takeover rumors surfaced on Monday, I sold the stock at 13.49. The stock hit my 14 target that day, too.

I made 25 percent in 5 days.

Did I sell too soon? Looking at the chart, it is easy to see that price continued to rise. However, it has been my experience that when a stock jumps on news by 5 to 20 percent or more, it is best to take profits. Often, the event day or the next price peaks and then drops for the rest of the month, sometimes giving back all of the gains and more.

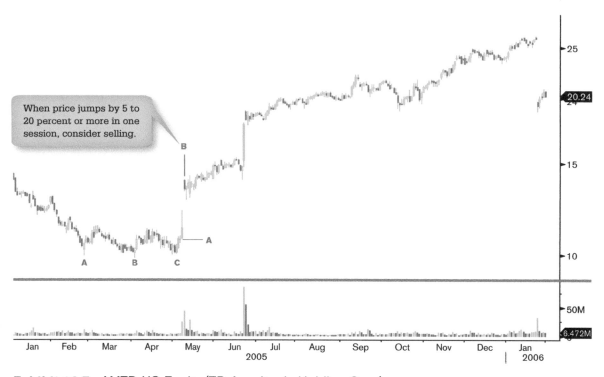

When price jumps by 5 to 20 percent or more in one session, consider selling.

Exhibit 18.7: AMTD US Equity (TD Ameritrade Holding Corp)

Performance

In all of the trades discussed so far, none of them used indicators like moving averages, RSI, or MACD. They used the basic setup, that of buying after the breakout and placing a stop below the bottom of the chart pattern.

How often does the basic setup work? The following table provides an answer for many of the chart patterns discussed in this book.

Test Yourself

Answer the following questions.

1. Why is placing a buy stop a penny above the top trendline in an ascending triangle important?
   A. It means price is going to trend.
   B. It signals a downward breakout.
   C. It prevents the order from executing when price stops at the top trendline.

2. What does "do not chase a stock" mean?
   A. Never fall in love with a stock.
   B. Buying too late can be hazardous to your wealth.
   C. Do not add to an existing position (scaling in).

3. Should you buy an unconfirmed double bottom?
   A. Only if you enjoy losing money.
   B. Yes, but only if the stock, industry, and market are trending in different directions.
   C. Yes, but recognize that the risk of failure increases.

Answers 1. C; 2. B; 3. C

CHAPTER 19

Failures

Chart patterns fail and they do so much too often. This chapter shows what some of those failures look like and gives hints on how to avoid them. The first hint is to buy stocks that only go up. If you can do that, then you do not need to read the rest of this chapter, and you can retire at 36 as I did.

Triangle Failures

For the rest of you mere mortals, imagine that you have a buy stop a penny above the top of the ascending triangle shown in Exhibit 19.1.

Price breaks out upward at A, and you are overjoyed at getting in on the ground floor of an advance.

Then, just three days later, your mood changes when price drops and busts the triangle for the first time. Fortunately, the stock remains above the bottom of the chart pattern where you have a stop loss order.

Price climbs above the top of the triangle and you are smiling again. The smile is brief because price drops, busting the pattern for the second time. This time, the stock drops far enough to hit your stop and take you out of the trade for a loss.

Almost as soon as the stock cashes you out, it turns, rises, and busts the triangle for the third time. In fact, the busting continues until the stock moves more than 10 percent away from the top of the triangle.

The exhibit shows what a triple busted ascending triangle looks like. Before trading ascending triangles, look for as many as you can find in the stocks you trade. See how price behaves. If they are as treacherous as this one, then look elsewhere.

Another Dud

Too many trades looks like this one. (See Exhibit 19.2.)

Price begins a long uptrend in late August (some of the move is not shown) and forms a descending triangle in the spring of 2011. Price breaks out upward at A and climbs for a time before reversing and busting

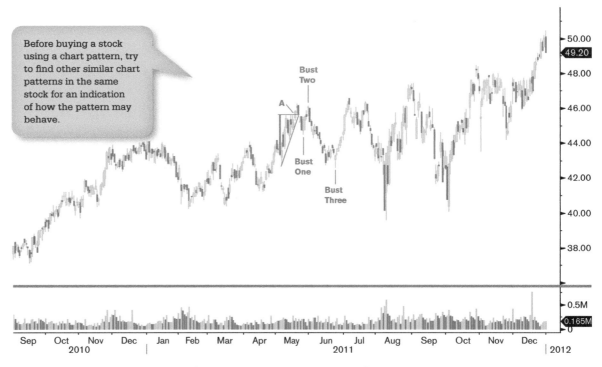

Exhibit 19.1: NJR US Equity (New Jersey Resources Corp)

the triangle when it closes below the bottom of the chart pattern.

How often does a bust occur? Answer: 22 percent of the time.

One key to this failure and others like it is the length of the upward price trend leading to the chart pattern. The earlier the chart pattern appears in that trend, the better.

A check of the numbers confirms this. Those chart patterns with a short-term period (less than three months) from the start of the trend to the chart pattern gain an average of 40 percent after an upward breakout. Those with an intermediate-term trend (three to six months) gain 37 percent, and those with a long-term trend (over six months) gain just 27 percent.

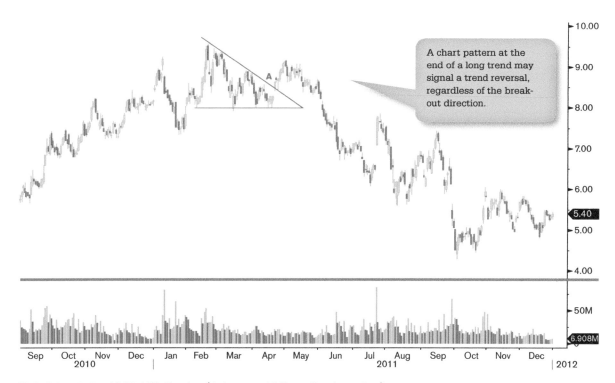

A chart pattern at the end of a long trend may signal a trend reversal, regardless of the break-out direction.

Exhibit 19.2: AMD US Equity (Advanced Micro Devices Inc)

Thus, look how far into the price trend the chart pattern appears. Expect that the longer the trend, the worse the performance.

Double Bottom Failures

When I looked at my spreadsheet of trades, much of what I saw was blood from double bottoms that failed

to produce a profit. One example of how that can happen is shown in Exhibit 19.3.

The downtrend begins at G on the far left of the chart. When the stock bottoms at double bottom AB, the stock had tumbled 38 percent. You might think the stock would be a buy at that level, especially when a double bottom reversal appears.

Exhibit 19.3: ACXM US Equity (Acxiom Corp)

The chart pattern confirms at C, so you buy the stock and set a stop a penny below B (the lower of the two bottoms), at 11.69. Price climbs to D and then trouble sets in.

The stock begins moving down, day after day it seems, bottoming at E. "Whew!" you say. "That was close!" Indeed it was since the stock bottomed at 11.74, a nickel above your stop. Price recovers along with your attitude and you are feeling good about the trade.

At F, the breakaway gap is a sign of good things to come. Those who wanted to buy after the throwback might buy at the open of candle F. You can do that with a buy stop a penny above the top of the chart pattern (C) placed sometime after E (after the throwback completed).

Those that bought in on candle F had all of a week to exit before the stock collapsed into loss territory. The stock continued down, hitting the stop to cash you out for a loss and bottoming at H, 24 percent below the stop and 53 percent below the high at G.

The moral of this story is manifold.

1. Not having a stop in place can be a bad decision.
2. It does not have to be a bear market before a stock loses a lot of money.
3. It can be difficult to determine when the market (or stock) bottoms.

Head-and-Shoulders Bottom Failures

As with any chart pattern, failures occur when price fails to trend in the expected direction. Exhibit 19.4 shows an example.

Let us begin with the measure rule to see what it says (I discuss how to use the measure rule in Chapter 24). The head low is at 5.71 and the neckline dot is at 14.38 for a height of 8.67. Added to the breakout price of 12.50, it says the target should be 21.17.

Does that make sense? No. Why not? Because the rise means a gain of 69 percent. That is much too high to be realistic. "But the stock reached the target!" I can hear you say. My reply: "Don't confuse the issue with facts!"

If you bought this stock at the breakout B or soon after, you may have placed a stop below the prior minor low. That would be below the right shoulder.

Those traders waiting for a throwback (C) would see D as the turn higher or even E and buy. They would probably use the low at D or E as the stop, only for a ride to the mortuary when their heart stopped as price collapsed to F.

If you were a courageous type, you may have placed a stop below the head. That would have worked in this case, but the potential loss was huge, 54 percent below the breakout! Three hundred joules. Clear!

This head-and-shoulders bottom forecasted the turn from bear market to bull. Three days after F, the general market turned bullish. The chart shows how tasty the recovery can be after a bear market ends.

Rectangle Failures

One failure of a rectangle top to perform up to expectations I show in Exhibit 19.5.

Price launches skyward at A and overshoots the start of the chart pattern at B. Then price moves sideways, but notice that the bottoms trend higher (blue trendline). This pattern is an ascending triangle, but the valleys are close enough to the trendline that it is fine as a rectangle top as well.

I say rectangle *top* and not a bottom because you should ignore overshoot (B) just before the chart

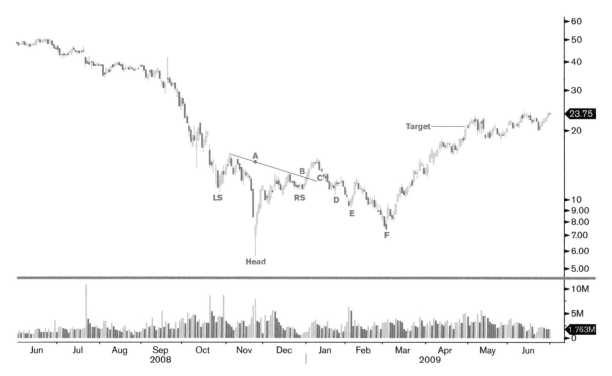

Exhibit 19.4: CE US Equity (Celanese Corp)

pattern. The price *trend* is upward leading to the chart pattern, not downward from the top of the one-day overshoot.

Price breaks out upward from the pattern at C, but then runs into trouble. The stock bumps its head against resistance at the price level of B and at the diamond top in February.

Look what happens next. The stock parachutes back to earth and lands at D, just above the launch price, A.

Notice how price climbed from E to the diamond top and then plummeted back to F on the exit. Was this a hint of how the rectangle would react? I will let you ponder that.

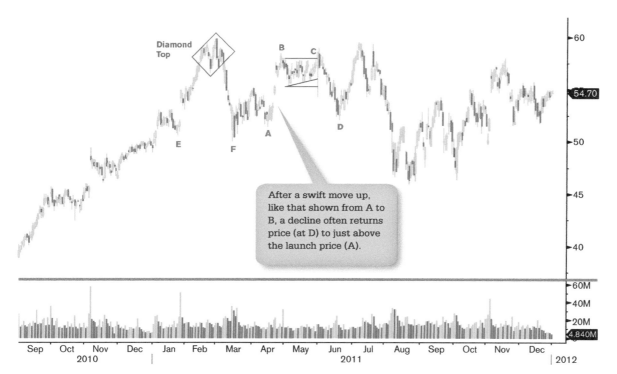

Within the chart:

Diamond Top

B   C

A

E   F

D

After a swift move up, like that shown from A to B, a decline often returns price (at D) to just above the launch price (A).

60

54.70

50

45

40

60M
40M
20M
4.840M

Sep Oct Nov Dec Jan Feb Mar Apr May Jun Jul Aug Sep Oct Nov Dec
2010   2011   2012

Exhibit 19.5: QCOM US Equity (QUALCOMM Inc)

Triple Bottom Failures

Why do triple bottoms fail to perform up to expectations? The answers can be many, but the simple fact is that price fails to trend.

Look at the triple bottom shown in Exhibit 19.6.

At E, a brokerage firm initiated coverage with an overweight recommendation. At F, the company an-nounced earnings that appeared to be better than expected. The next day, the stock gaped upward to D but then sentiment changed. The stock slid down a hill from D in a straight line until hitting trees in the form of triple bottom ABC.

The ABC pattern confirmed when price closed above the red line, but the reversal failed to spin price

KEY POINT:
Chart patterns fail when price does not trend.

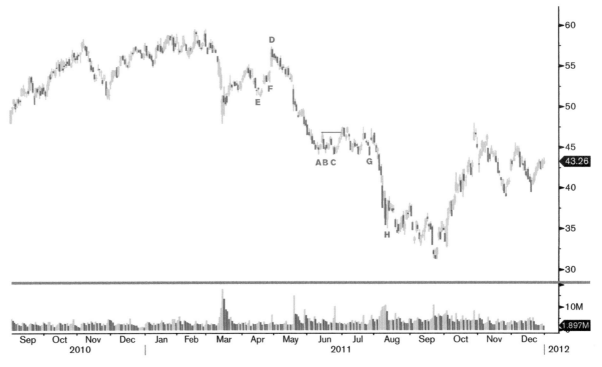

Exhibit 19.6: AFL US Equity (Aflac Inc)

upward. A stop placed below the bottom of this chart pattern would have limited the pain.

The triple bottom was supposed to act as a reversal—and it did—but only for two months. Another earnings announcement at G saw price move higher for a few days, starting with an area gap. The forces that pushed price down from D came back and punished the stock again, sending it lower going into the fall.

Notice how small the ABC pattern was. Since we know that small patterns tend to underperform their larger brothers, this could be a clue to this situation, especially combined with the strong run down from D (a straight line).

This triple bottom acted as a half-staff pattern appearing midway from D to H.

Option B: Price forms a higher peak and higher valley.

Option C: Price rises above the highest peak between the breakout and throwback low.

Option A. If you wait for price to *close* above the top of the chart pattern again (after a throwback), then that is a good way to determine price has recovered from the throwback. That happens at D in Exhibit 20.1.

This is a good method because the chart pattern can act as overhead resistance, so if price drops too far during a throwback, it might hit that overhead resistance and then turn back down. Waiting for it to punch through that resistance removes that concern.

Buying at D also gets you into the trade at a good price. It is as if you bought near the original breakout price.

Option B. Another way to determine throwback completion is to trail a buy stop above a prior minor high as price drops during the throwback. For example, place an initial buy stop above E. When price drops below the blue line (drawn from the low after E, to the right), lower the buy stop to G or F. Keep lowering the buy stop as price drops, but remember that the chart pattern still poses overhead resistance.

Waiting for price to rise above the lowest peak will result in a failed trade if the primary trend switches to down. Keep that in mind.

Option C. The last option is to wait for price to recover completely and begin making new highs. Find the highest peak between the breakout (B) and the lowest low during the throwback (C). That would be E. When price closes above E, buy the stock.

A scan of a hundred or so ascending triangles shows that waiting for the throwback to clear the peak at E often has the best results. Unfortunately, this method also gets you into the stock at a high price.

Double Bottom Throwbacks

Some traders find it smart to wait for a throwback before trading a chart pattern. That way, they eliminate situations like that shown in Exhibit 20.2.

A and B are the twin valleys of a double bottom chart pattern. When price closes above C, it confirms the double bottom as a valid pattern. If you bought then and placed a stop loss order below bottom B, you would have been stopped out on the throwback plunge to D.

By waiting for the throwback to complete, I sidestepped that calamity and bought the stock when it became clear that the uptrend had resumed.

At the time, the yield on holding the utility stock was 5.4 percent. I placed a stop at a split-adjusted price of 19, below the buy price of 20.31, and below the spike at D.

Fast forward to March, with interest rates rising; I tucked my stop under support at 26.67, which the stock hit. During the hold time, I collected three dividend payments and made 35 percent.

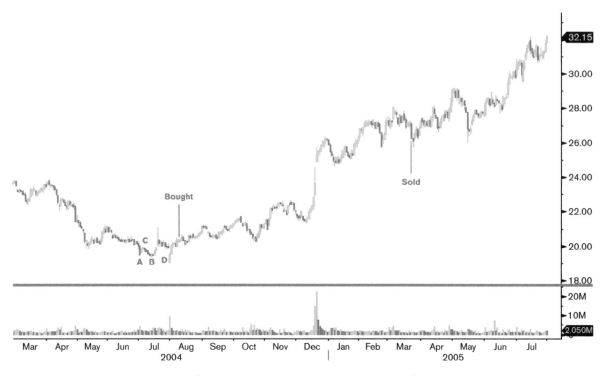

Exhibit 20.2: PEG US Equity (Public Service Enterprise Group Inc)

Pre-Throwback Setup for Double Bottoms

This variation of the throwback setup is for advanced traders. Exhibit 20.3 shows a double bottom at AB that confirms at C when the stock gaps upward.

The idea for this setup is to buy as soon as possible and ride the move up to the top, D, where the throwback begins. How do you do that?

Setup Rules:

1. Count the number of higher closes approaching what you believe will be a breakout day. If it is less

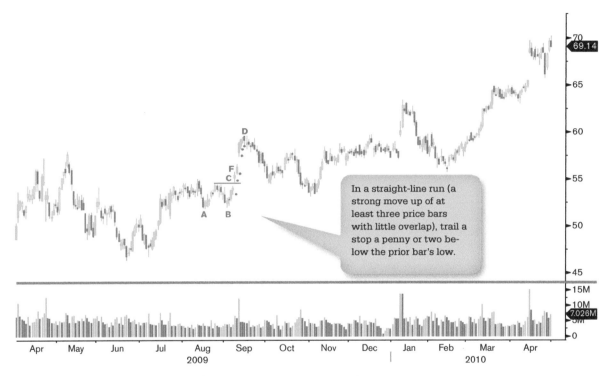

In a straight-line run (a strong move up of at least three price bars with little overlap), trail a stop a penny or two below the prior bar's low.

Exhibit 20.3: UPS US Equity (United Parcel Service Inc)

than three, skip the trade. In other words, look for three higher closes in the three days immediately before a breakout.

2. Place a buy stop at the confirmation price.
3. After the order triggers, place a stop below the prior candle's low.
4. Trail the stop higher by raising it each day as a higher low appears.

It will be rare that price will shoot out of the chart pattern as it does in Exhibit 20.3 . However, when it does, you will be ready with this setup.

For the first step, look at the days leading to the breakout. If price is making a series of higher closes, as it is in this example, expect a strong breakout.

Research says that the likelihood of a throwback drops to 30 percent if price makes three higher closes in the days immediately before the breakout day. In this example, the three days begin with the red candle the day after B (this is difficult to see on the chart) and ends the day before the breakout. The breakout (C) is the fourth higher close.

Enter the trade at the open of candle C.

Place a stop below the prior candle's low. I show that with the lowest red dot. The next day, candle F appears. Raise the stop to the dot a penny below C. With each passing day, raise the stop as the red dots show. Eventually, the stop gets hit at D.

If a price bar is unusually tall (intraday, before the market closes for the day), say two or three times the average height of bars over the prior month (20 price bars), then either sell as close to the high as you can or raise the stop to a penny below midway on the tall bar. Why? Because within a day or so of a tall candle, price often reverses. Try to capture as much of that tall candle's gain before selling.

If a straight-line run does not emerge, then look back at the throwback statistics and exhibits in Chapter 6. Try exiting using time. The *median* time for price to peak before throwing back is four days. Then the return trip starts. You may want to exit on day four.

A frequency distribution of the gain from the breakout price to the throwback peak shows that the stock peaks in the following order: 6, 8, 4, 10 percent, and then the other values (at two percentage point intervals) in smaller denominations. In other words,

the stock tends to rise 6 percent the most in a throwback. In second place, the stock rises 8 percent. Third place is 4 percent and so on. Use those percentages as guides to what you can expect when price breaks out upward.

If you see a large price overlap, then a reversal could be next. Use Bollinger bands and look for a low volatility day. If the bands narrow considerably, then expect a more volatile day (meaning a potential reversal with a large price swing as volatility increases).

Play with this setup on paper to see if you can scalp some bucks from the breakout.

Pre-Throwback Setup for Rectangles

Exhibit 20.4 shows a setup I developed for rectangles that capitalizes on price behavior before a throwback.

The exhibit shows a rectangle bottom with an upward breakout. The setup buys the breakout and sells at either a 5 percent gain or after three price bars. No stop is used.

Here are the rules for this setup.

1. Stocks under $5 excluded.
2. Place a buy stop a penny above the top of the chart pattern.
3. If the order executes, exit if price rises 5 percent above the buy price.
4. Otherwise, exit at the close three bars later.

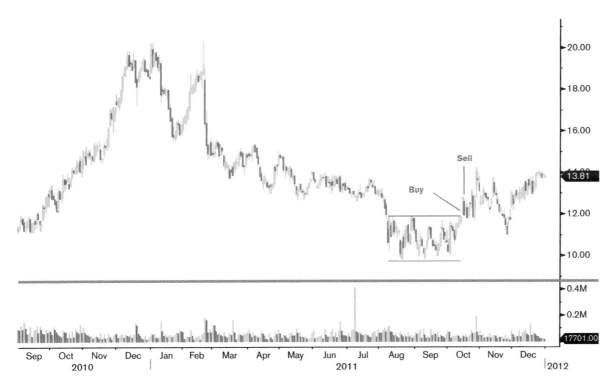

Exhibit 20.4: CDI US Equity (CDI Corp)

The exhibit shows how the setup works. Entry occurs when price gaps above the top of the rectangle, so the buy price is the opening price, $11.98. Five percent above this is $12.58. I did not allow an exit on the first day, but that is a software coding issue. The earliest exit will occur at the open the next day.

The next day, the opening price is 12.62, which is more than 5 percent above the target price. The trade exits at that time. If price fails to climb at least 5 percent, then the trade would exit three price bars after entry (on bar four).

FAST FACTS

Rectangles throw back between 59 percent (rectangle bottoms) and 64 percent (rectangle tops) of the time in a bull market.

How well does this work? I tested 1,001 rectangles with upward breakouts and found the following.

	Result Summary
Number of trades	1,001
Win/loss	77%
Average profit/loss	$253.03 or 2.5%
Maximum loss	−12%
Average win	311.59 or 3.1%
Average loss	−$58.55 or −0.6%
Price exit trades	433
Price exit profit	$583.57 or 5.8%
Time exit trades	568
Time exit profit	$1.05 or 1.1%

Each trade used $10,000 to buy a stock with $10 commissions per trade ($20 round trip). The setup wins 77 percent of the time, making an average of $253. The largest loss was 12 percent.

When the setup exited because price had climbed at least 5 percent, the setup made $583 and exited using that method 433 times. The other 568 exits were because time reached the three-bar limit. The average time limited trade made just $1.05. That suggests a search for a more optimum time exit is advisable.

A check of four days showed that the results were worse. The time exit trades posted an average loss of $1.59. At two days, the time-limited trades gained $13.17. Shorter is the way to go, especially since it cuts the drawdown and market exposure. However, it also cuts profits. The average win drops to $283 from $312.

Notice that the setup does not use any fancy indicators and yet generates a respectable return over the testing period from July 1991 to November 2011. That covers two bear markets and three bull ones.

The next chapter discusses using the measure rule for flags and pennants. Those half-staff patterns can signal when it is time to exit the trading party before the police arrive.

Test Yourself

Answer the following.

1. Which, if any, of the following statements are true?

   A. A throwback occurs only after an upward breakout.

   B. On average, the appearance of a throwback suggests worse performance.

   C. On average, performance suffers if price drops too far during the throwback.

2. True or false: Double bottoms never have throwbacks because they are bottom patterns, not tops.

3. True or false: An unusually tall price bar means price will peak or valley soon, but their appearance is no guarantee.

Answers: 1. A, B, C; 2. False; 3. True

CHAPTER 21

Measuring Flags and Pennants

This chapter explains how the measure rule applies to flags and pennants, and how traders can use it to predict a trend change.

Traders knowledgeable about flags and pennants know them as half-staff patterns. That means they can appear midway in a price trend. Let me explain using Exhibit 21.1.

The position of pennant BC is about midway in trend AD. Since you know the length of the flagpole (AB), you can project the price where the trend could end. It does not always work, of course, but flags and pennants are handy when you need to determine a trend's lifetime.

The Measure Rule

If BC is the midpoint in the price trend, then we can project where the stock will end its run. Here is how it is done.

Measure the height of the flagpole from the start of the pole (A) to its end (B). The end of the pole is the highest high at the start of the flag or pennant. In this case, A is at a low of 57.14 and B is at a high of 64.47 for a height of 7.33. Add the height to the low price at the end of the pennant (the day before the breakout), C (62.00), to get a conservative estimate of 69.33.

I show the target with a horizontal blue line.

To make this process clear, here are the steps.

1. Measure the height of the flagpole from the low price at the start of the trend (bottom of the flagpole) to the high price at the end of the trend (top of the pole). The top of the pole is at the start of the flag or pennant.
2. Add the height to the low price just before the new trend breaks out of the flag or pennant.
3. The result is the target price.

Let us run through the next pennant and see what the measure rule predicts. The flagpole begins at

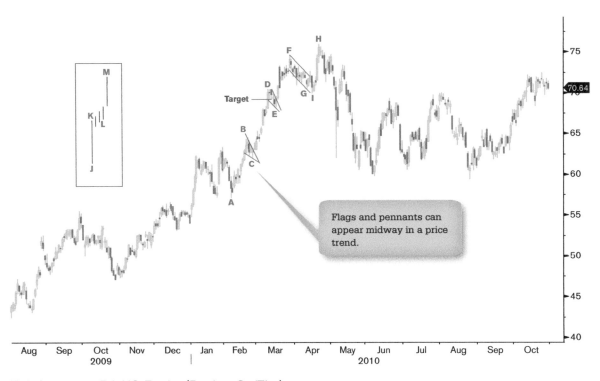

Flags and pennants can appear midway in a price trend.

Exhibit 21.1: BA US Equity (Boeing Co/The)

C (62.00) and climbs to a high of 70.48 at D, for a height of 8.48. Add this to the low at E (68.30) for a target of 76.78. The high at H is 76.00, so the measure rule fails in this example by 78 cents.

Another example: For the next flag, the flagpole begins at E (68.30) and rises to a high of 74.53 at F for a height of 6.23. Add this to the bottom of the flag at

G (70.50) for a target of 76.73. Again, price falls short of the target.

If you look at the size of flag FG in comparison to the height of the flagpole (EF), the price trend bends because of the weight. I would use a longer flagpole (CF) to support this flag, and lengthen the flag to include the low at I in the measure rule. That does

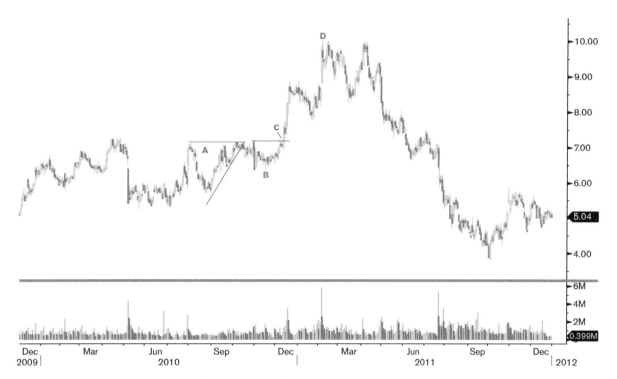

Exhibit 22.2: HLIT US Equity (Harmonic Inc)

on the opposite side of the chart pattern and then gets stopped out.

Busted Ascending Triangles

Exhibit 22.2 shows an example of a single busted ascending triangle.

This is not an ideal ascending triangle because of the white space at A. Price squeezes out the apex of the triangle, staging a downward breakout, but price does not drop far, to B—less than 10 percent—before heading up.

When price closes above the top of the triangle at C, it busts the downward breakout. That would be the time to buy the stock. In this example, price tops out at D, over 40 percent above the breakout price.

Here are the rules for trading busted patterns with downward breakouts.

1. Price breaks out downward from a chart pattern.
2. The stock drops 10 percent or less and then reverses direction.
3. Price closes above the top of the chart pattern.
4. Buy at the open the next day.

How often do ascending triangles bust? Answer: 40 percent of the time. That means 40 percent of the time, an ascending triangle with a *downward* breakout will see price drop less than 10 percent before recovering and closing above the top of the chart pattern.

After that, price rises an average of 26 percent, but that includes double and triple busted patterns. The number compares to an average rise of 34 percent for ascending triangles with upward breakouts. If you compare single busted performance only, the gains are larger: 40 percent instead of 26 percent.

The results say that trading upward breakouts is best, but when you see a downward breakout that reverses quickly, buying it can be as exciting as discovering that the birds have not yet pecked into your ripe tomatoes (that is a problem in my garden, but so are spider mites).

FAST FACTS

Twenty-nine percent of busted descending triangles with downward breakouts are single busts, 6 percent are double busts, and 6 percent bust at least three times.

Busted Descending Triangles

A busted descending triangle means a downward breakout followed by price closing above the top of the triangle. I show that scenario in Exhibit 22.3.

Two red lines bound the descending triangle tighter than a calf at a rodeo roping contest, and the stock breaks out downward at A. Price drops less than 10 percent before reversing direction and closing above the top of the chart pattern. That happens at B. Buy at the open the next day.

At C, the company announces earnings that are as exciting to traders as chocolate Easter bunnies are to kids (and adults).

A full 40 percent of descending triangles with downward breakouts bust at least once. The average rise after busting above the top of the triangle is 29 percent.

The results are based on perfect trades using 250 busted descending triangles, so do not expect to duplicate the results in actual trading.

Busted Symmetrical Triangles

Until I studied busted chart patterns, I thought that symmetrical triangles double busted frequently. I was right. In other words, the up and down price action that forms the symmetrical triangle can continue after the breakout, making it difficult to profit from them.

Exhibit 22.3: BSET US Equity (Bassett Furniture Industries Inc)

Exhibit 22.4 shows an example of a single busted symmetrical triangle that leads to a good move.

Price broke out downward from the chart pattern at A when price closed below the bottom trendline. The stock did not drop far before reversing. Price busted the triangle when it closed above the top of the chart pattern at B. The gap, C, was a breakaway gap that predicted a strong move up.

Buying at the open at B would have gotten you in at 62.44. If you were to exit at peak E, 71.79, you would have made 15 percent in about six weeks. That represents a perfect trade, of course.

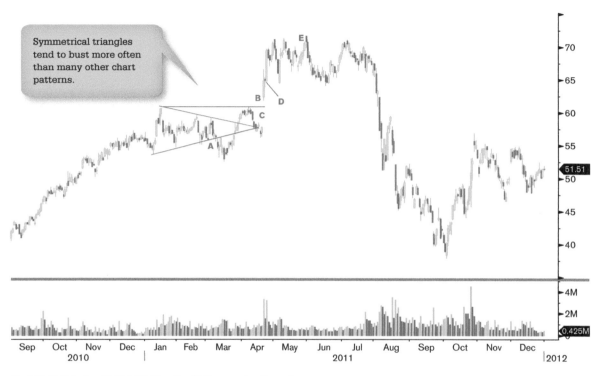

> Symmetrical triangles tend to bust more often than many other chart patterns.

Exhibit 22.4: ALB US Equity (Albemarle Corp)

Busted Double Tops

For the next busted setup, I have to switch to double tops, which Exhibit 22.5 shows.

The double top is at AB and it confirms when price closes below the red line at C. Price drops to D, which is less than 10 percent below the breakout price, before the stock rebounds.

The stock climbs to E where it busts the pattern for the first time. Price stalls at overhead resistance setup by the double top peaks and heads back down.

When it closes below the bottom of the double top at F, it busts the pattern for the second time. It finishes busting the double top for the third time when it closes above the double top. Only then did price trend.

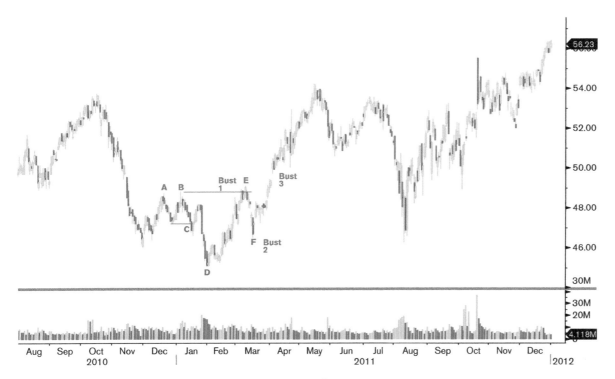

Exhibit 22.5: ABT US Equity (Abbott Laboratories)

Of course, this is an example of how awful trading busted patterns can be. If you had a stop in place above the top of the double top, you would have taken a loss on the first bust.

Fortunately, double and triple busts are quite rare. For double tops, they happen 5 percent of the time, each, for double and triple busts. Single busts, by comparison, happen 23 percent of the time in a bull market.

Busted Head-and-Shoulders Tops

Exhibit 22.6 shows an example of a busted head-and-shoulders top that appears at the end of a downward price trend.

Price breaks out downward when it closes below the red neckline at A. The stock eases lower for two

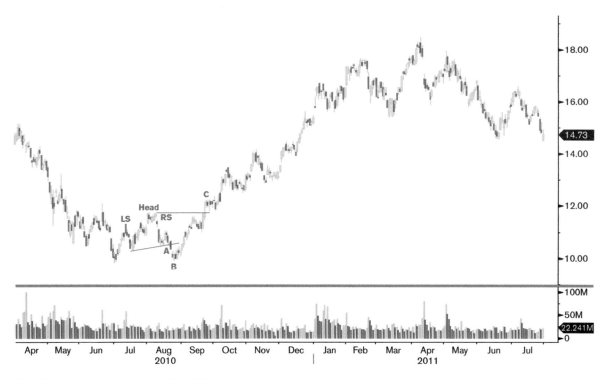

Exhibit 22.6: **AA US Equity (Alcoa Inc)**

more days before beginning a recovery. That recovery sees price close above the top of the chart pattern at C. When it does that, it busts the head-and-shoulders top. You can see the delicious gain that resulted.

Here are the setup rules for trading busted head-and-shoulders tops.

1. Look for a confirmed head-and-shoulders top.

2. Price drops less than 10 percent below the breakout price before reversing direction.

3. The stock *closes* above the highest peak in the chart pattern.

4. Buy the stock at the open the next day.

5. Place a stop loss order below the lowest valley in the head-and-shoulders.

You may be wondering why I do not include basic indicators like the 50-day or 200-day simple moving average (SMA) in my setups. The answer is because they do not provide any value.

For example, I tested the above setup with a 50-day SMA and found that out of 479 trades, just eight had the breakout price below the moving average. Those eight resulted in gains of 51 percent compared to 31 percent for those above the SMA.

The 200-day SMA showed similar results. Out of 472 trades, 31 were below the moving average and they showed gains of 44 percent. Those with breakouts above the moving average had gains of 30 percent.

The sample counts of those below the moving averages are too small to be reliable, but they hint that when busted patterns act as bullish reversals, they outperform. In other words, when you test a moving average like the 200-day, see if your results improve if price is *below* the moving average and not above it.

Busted Rectangles

Exhibit 22.7 shows a busted rectangle top. Price breaks out downward and bottoms at A before reversing and closing above the top of the chart pattern.

I also show this chart for another reason. Notice that the rectangle appears midway in the BC run. When trading chart patterns, remember that the pattern could appear halfway in the trend.

Rectangle bottoms perform better than tops with this setup in a bull market, with gains averaging 37 percent versus 30 percent, respectively. That is for perfect trades, but it serves as a good comparison.

Busted Triple Tops

For the next busted pattern, we have to use triple tops to buy an upward move. Exhibit 22.8 shows two examples of what I mean.

Triple top ABC has a downward breakout that bottoms at G. Notice that the drop is less than 10 percent below the lowest valley in the triple top (the red line).

Price climbs and closes above the top of the triple top at H. That is when the stock busts for the first time.

The second triple top, DEF, shows a similar scenario. Price confirms the pattern when it closes below the red line. The stock does not drop far before reversing and closing above the blue line to the right of F. I drew that line starting from the highest peak in the chart pattern. When price closed above that line at I, it busted the downward breakout.

The gap is a breakaway gap, so in this case, that would mean buying into this setup at the open a day after I. For the ABC pattern, buy at the open a day after H.

Place a stop below the bottom of the chart pattern and then pray.

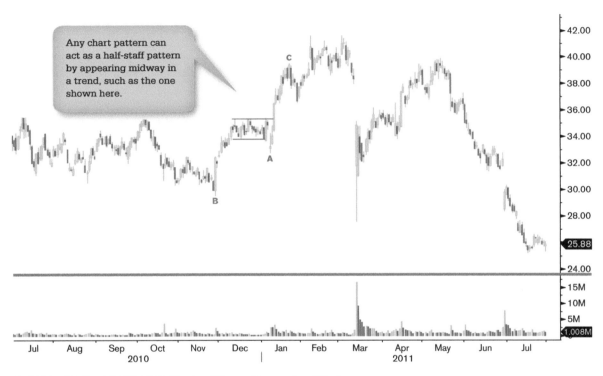

Any chart pattern can act as a half-staff pattern by appearing midway in a trend, such as the one shown here.

Exhibit 22.7: SHAW US Equity (Shaw Group Inc/The)

Performance

We breezed through the various busted chart patterns that break out downward and bust upward. Using the setup rules already described, the following table shows how often a busted pattern reaches a profit target (sorted by the 10% column).

Busted Chart Pattern	5%	10%	15%	20%
Descending triangles	82%	70%	61%	55%
Symmetrical triangles	82%	69%	58%	52%
Head-and-shoulders tops	81%	68%	57%	51%
Ascending triangles	79%	66%	57%	52%

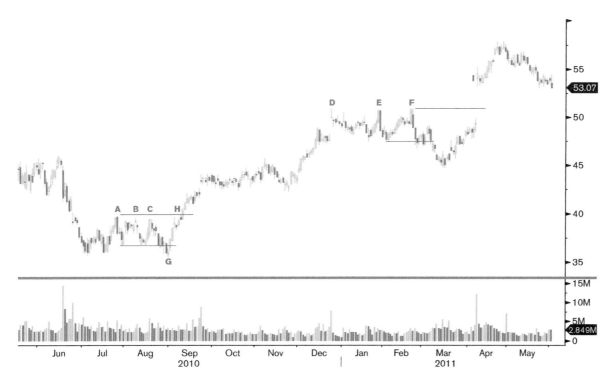

Exhibit 22.8: BBBY US Equity (Bed Bath & Beyond Inc)

Busted Chart Pattern	5%	10%	15%	20%
Double tops	82%	66%	57%	48%
Rectangles	78%	65%	54%	44%
Triple tops	80%	64%	56%	49%

For example, busted descending triangles, those with downward breakouts that bust upward, show price climbing at least 10 percent above the top of the chart pattern 70 percent of the time. By this measure, descending triangles are the best performing of the bunch.

What the number means is that if you wait for price to bust the triangle, you have a 70 percent chance of making at least 10 percent, and a 55 percent chance of making at least 20 percent.

The worst performance is for triple tops that show only 64 percent of the busted patterns rising at least 10 percent above the highest peak in the triple top.

Busted How Often?

How often does a chart pattern double or triple bust? The following table answers that, sorted by the double-busted column.

Chart Pattern Busts	Single	Double	Triple	Total
Head-and-shoulders tops	20%	4%	4%	28%
Double tops	23%	5%	5%	33%
Triple tops	24%	6%	7%	37%
Descending triangles	29%	6%	6%	40%
Ascending triangles	27%	6%	7%	40%
Rectangles	28%	5%	9%	42%
Symmetrical triangles	30%	7%	6%	42%

For example, head-and-shoulders tops have the fewest single busts of all of the patterns in the table. They also double and triple bust less often than their peers. When you include round-off error in the numbers, they bust 28 percent of the time.

At the bottom of the table, symmetrical triangles single bust 30 percent of the time and double bust the most, too. They tie with rectangles for busting the most often, 42 percent of the time. That is why it can be so difficult trading symmetrical triangles. You buy an upward breakout only to see the triangle bust, cashing you out for a loss and probably raising your blood pressure, too.

Notice that the bump patterns, head-and-shoulders, double and triple tops, are at the top of the table and those based on trendlines, triangles and rectangles, are at the bottom. What does this mean? I have no idea.

Actually, it gives a hint that for busted and non-busted chart patterns, stick to those with bumps and not trendlines.

Busted Versus Non-Busted Performance

The final table shows the performance of busted and non-busted patterns with downward breakouts that

Busted Chart Pattern, Downward Breakout	All Busted Types	Single Busted	Non-Busted
Rectangles	34%	61%	33%
Head-and-shoulders tops/bottoms	31%	42%	37%
Descending triangles	29%	45%	35%
Triple tops/bottoms	29%	43%	32%
Double tops/bottoms	28%	38%	38%
Symmetrical triangles	28%	41%	29%
Ascending triangles	26%	40%	34%

In fact, when price curls over and attempts to throw back but remains above the breakout price, performance improves. Throwbacks that plunge too far result in performance worse than do those with shallow plunges.

This makes intuitive sense because a throwback robs the stock of upward momentum. Stocks with shallow throwbacks retain more upward momentum.

Height and Width

Tall double bottoms perform better than short ones, with gains averaging 44 percent to 34 percent. What is meant by "tall"? Take the height of the chart pattern, from highest peak to lowest valley, and divide the height by the breakout price. If the result is above 15.6 percent (the median value), then it is a tall double bottom; otherwise, it is short.

If you want to add in width, then patterns wider than 37 days perform better, too, with gains averaging 42 percent to 34 percent.

In each tip, the numbers are averages of perfectly traded double bottoms. You may find a double bottom that is tall and wide, has no throwback, and has a short-term trend leading down to it. Then price rises just 5 percent. The next day, the company announces earnings worse than expected and sees the stock drop 67 percent in one session.

A stock I owned, Michaels Stores, dropped between 20 percent and 49 percent in one session 18 different times. I fought back and rode that stock from a split

adjusted price of 88 cents to $44, a return of almost 5,000 percent. It took 16 years.

If you trade often enough, the percentages described here should work to your benefit. Of course, if you are a terrible trader and decide to quit, then maybe they will let you return to the bomb disposal squad.

Seven Trading Clues for Head-and-Shoulders

The head-and-shoulders bottom provides plenty of performance clues that help predict how well the stock will perform after the breakout. The following is from a study of 1,600 head-and-shoulders bottoms, between mid-1991 and late 2011. They represent perfect trades, so do not expect your results to equal those discussed here. Use the numbers only for comparison purposes.

For the best performance, look for:

1. A short-term (zero to three months) downtrend leading to the left shoulder.

Find the trend start that leads to the left shoulder. The trend start is the highest high or lowest low before which the stock climbed (before the lowest low) or dropped (before the highest high) by at least 20 percent.

If the time between the trend start and the left shoulder valley is less than three months, the gains average 40 percent. Intermediate-term trends (three to six months) show gains of 36% and long-term trends (over six months) result in gains of 33 percent.

2. Down-sloping neckline.

Patterns with down-sloping necklines gain 40 percent versus 31 percent for those with up-sloping necklines.

3. Tall patterns.

Tall head-and-shoulders bottoms, measured from the highest peak to the lowest valley, outperform short ones. This is also true of most chart patterns, not just head-and-shoulders bottoms.

In the case of a head-and-shoulders bottom, patterns taller than the median 15 percent, which is the height divided by the breakout price, show gains averaging 49 percent. Those shorter than the median have gains of just 28 percent.

Pattern height is one of the key indicators of performance.

4. Wide patterns.

Head-and-shoulders bottoms wider than the median 41 days show gains averaging 44 percent compared to narrower patterns that show gains of 30 percent.

Head-and-shoulders both tall and wide show gains averaging 51 percent! Check your pulse. Do not get too excited. Remember, these numbers are for perfect trades, buying at the breakout price and selling at the highest peak before price tumbles—and doing it hundreds of times.

5. High right shoulder volume.

When the right shoulder volume is above the left shoulder and head, the stocks gain 48 percent (versus gains averaging 36 percent for volume highest on the head and 32 percent for high left shoulder volume).

6. High breakout day volume.

Those head-and-shoulders with breakout day volume higher than the one-month average have gains averaging 40 percent. Those with wimpy volume gain 30 percent.

7. No throwbacks.

Head-and-shoulders bottoms without throwbacks gain 42 percent, on average. Those with throwbacks gain 33 percent.

Monthly Symmetrical Triangle Setup

Tall symmetrical triangles mean better performance. I tested this and found it to be true with tall triangles showing post breakout gains averaging 39 percent and short ones averaging 24 percent (627 samples each). Again, those numbers are for perfect trades, so do not expect to achieve these results.

What if we use the monthly scale and trade triangles? I used data from 1998 to 2006 on hundreds of stocks and looked for symmetrical triangles on the monthly chart. Some of these can be funky looking and it takes some getting used to. Often you will be working with two trendline touches on at least one side. One example is shown in Exhibit 23.1.

The triangle has two trendline touches on the top and three on the bottom (including one near miss).

Exhibit 23.1: WAT US Equity (Waters Corp)

It breaks out upward at A, peaks at B, and then falls at the start of a bear market. If you draw trendline C beneath price as it climbs, you could sell on a trendline pierce. A safer mechanism is to wait for a close below the trendline and sell at the open the next month. I show that at D.

If you bought at A (45.13) and sold at D (57.57), you would have made 28 percent. If you sold at peak B (81.84), you would have made 81 percent. If you set a hard exit to sell at 20 percent down from a peak, you would have captured a profit of 45 percent.

The system I used to calculate gains would find the ultimate high at B and use that as the exit price. It represents a perfect trade. After that, price dropped by at least 20 percent, measured from monthly high to close. The high to *close* method is important on the monthly scale because it ignores the fluctuations during the month.

Testing using this method showed that the 129 monthly symmetrical triangles in bull markets with upward breakouts gained an average of 111 percent. Just two gained 8 percent and 9 percent, with 81 percent of the triangles gaining more than 45 percent.

Here are guidelines that may make trading monthly triangles easier. Since this is a buy-and-hold setup, no stops are used.

1. Use the monthly *log* scale to find symmetrical triangles.
2. Look for at least two touches of one trendline and preferably three or more of the other.
3. Place a buy stop a few cents above the top trendline.
4. After getting into the trade, let price run. If it trends, draw a trendline beneath price. A close below the trendline is an exit signal. Sell at the open the next month.
5. If price rises well above the trendline, then draw a new one to hug price better, or sell if price drops 20 percent from the highest peak.
6. If you double your money, then place a stop at a gain of 100 percent. Almost half of the triangles (47 percent) doubled in price, but it takes an average of 1 year and 9 months to make those gains.
7. If price ever closes the month more than 20 percent below the purchase price, sell.

You can use the measure rule (see Chapter 24) in the normal manner. Price hit the target 81 percent of the time.

Rectangles

Are you a swinger? Swing trader, that is. If so, then maybe rectangles are for you. Buy near the bottom trendline and sell near the top, sit back and collect money. It is not that easy, of course. Exhibit 23.2 shows an intra-formation setup for rectangles with upward breakouts.

Price bounces between two horizontal trendlines, touching the bottom at AB and the top at CD. Once those four touches printed on the chart, then a swing trader on the prowl could sell short at D and F, cover and go long at E and G, and then exit at H. After that, click your heels three times and say, "I did not short at H"; otherwise, you may be searching the couch cushions for bus fare back to Kansas.

A swinger late to the party would have fewer trading opportunities, of course. This rectangle is just over $2 tall, but bouncing from $5 to $7 a share, the trades represent a hefty 40 percent gain for long trades and 29 percent for the short ones.

Here are the setup rules.

1. Find a rectangle: two peaks that top out near the same price and two valleys that bottom near the same price.
2. Measure the height between the peaks and valleys. Can you make enough money trading between them to justify the risk?
3. Short/sell near the top of the rectangle and cover/buy near the bottom.
4. Place stops outside the rectangle far enough to avoid being stopped out on normal price action.

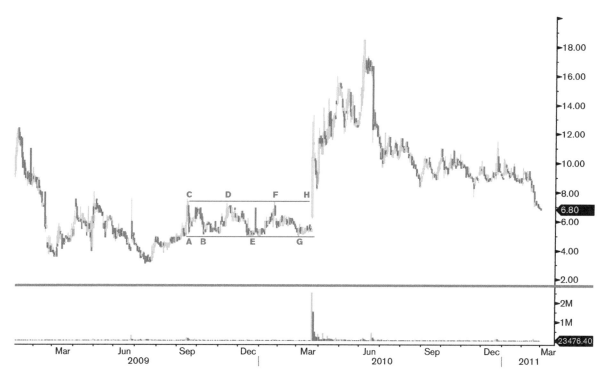

Exhibit 23.2: ARWR US Equity (Arrowhead Research Corp)

The rectangle has to last tall enough to make profitable swings, and finding a tradable rectangle to begin with is about as easy as bowling strikes.

My experience says that as soon as you find a repeatable pattern, it stops repeating. Tradable rectangles, like the one shown in the exhibit, are rare and should be attempted only by experienced traders with a death wish.

The next chapter begins a discussion of selling. It does not matter at what price you buy a stock. What matters is the selling price.

Let me offer this piece of advice. If you just focus on technique (planning the trade and trading the plan) instead of money, you will make more with less stress.

KEY POINT:

Before placing an intra-formation trade, make sure the chart pattern is tall enough to be worth the risk. If price stops short of the target, have a plan to exit.

Test Yourself

Answer the following.

1. True or false: On a breakout from a chart pattern, price often shoots through nearby (say, within 5 percent of the breakout price) support and resistance.

2. Which, if any, of the following support or resistance features could impede price movement after a chart pattern breakout?

   A. Horizontal consolidation regions
   B. Minor highs or lows
   C. Trendlines
   D. Whole numbers
   E. All of the above

3. True or false: Short chart patterns are like concentrated energy drinks. They pack a more powerful punch than tall patterns (that is, price tends to move farther after the breakout from a short pattern).

Answers: 1. True; 2. A, B, C; 3. False

PART IV

BASIC SELL SIGNALS

Deciding when to sell is as hard as making up your mind and pulling the trigger. That decision-making process can be made easier by using chart patterns. They offer advantages that other techniques do not.

For example, a confirmed bearish chart pattern is a sell signal, and I will introduce you to seven of them.

But not all bearish chart patterns mean a substantial decline. That is when the measure rule helps.

Use the measure rule to estimate how far price is going to fall. If the drop is severe enough, then you know to sell now and save losing your shirt for another time.

CHAPTER 24

Chart Pattern Sell Signals

This chapter takes a brief tour through several chart patterns, looking for sell signals. With each one, we apply the measure rule to predict how far price will tumble, look for underlying support, and determine if the move is worth avoiding.

Selling Ascending Triangles

Suppose that you own the stock shown in Exhibit 24.1. Should you sell at D?

The decision to sell or hold is important because you face it on every trade. Let us read this chart to see how we can decide.

An ascending triangle appears in red. When price closes below the up-sloping trendline, it is a sell signal. If we are a day trader or swing trader, then our choice is easy: Sell immediately.

However, if we are a buy-and-hold investor or position trader looking for a home run, why would we want to sell? We want to hold the stock unless price is going to make a dramatic move downward.

To help determine how far price is going to drop, we can use the measure rule. Take the height of most chart patterns and add it to the breakout price for upward breakouts or subtract it from the breakout price for downward breakouts. The result is the target price.

For example, the height of the triangle is A − B or 1.83. That predicts a 4.5 percent drop below the breakout price (D, 40.97) to 39.14. I show the target as a horizontal red line at E.

The target reaches the support area shown circled at F. F is a horizontal consolidation region; although price is not horizontal, it does show lots of overlap.

A drop to G, the launch price, is also possible. A drop that far would mean a 9 percent decline. For holding a long-term position, I am more worried about visiting my dentist (the dentist I had when growing up never used Novocain; watch the movie *Marathon Man* and you will understand) than a 9 percent decline.

DEFINITION:

Position trader

A trader who holds positions from weeks to months, seeking to ride the trend until it ends, is called a position trader.

KEY POINT:

The measure rule for downward breakouts from ascending triangles works in a manner similar to upward breakouts. Take the height of the triangle from the highest peak to the lowest valley in the chart pattern and subtract the height from the breakout price to get a target. The breakout price is where the stock pierces the up-sloping trendline. Price hits the target 58 percent of the time.

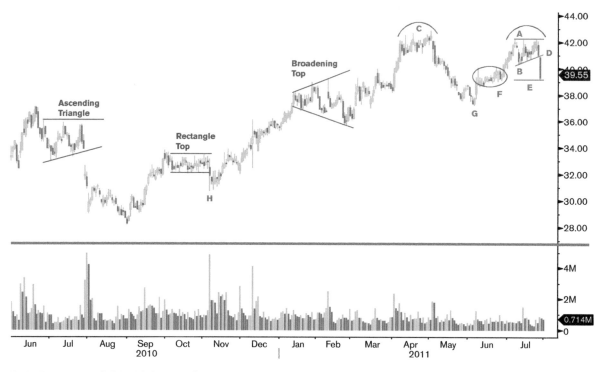

Exhibit 24.1: CRL US Equity (Charles River Laboratories International Inc)

The broadening top in early 2011, which appears as a loose congestion area, may act as support and help stop the drop. I do not have much faith in loose congestion areas because price has a tendency to stream right through them like water draining through a colander. Tight areas work much better.

The big worry is the double top. I show that with two blue arcs at A and C. The measure rule says that this pattern will see price drop to 31.66 (midway between H and the rectangle's bottom). From the low at D, that is a painful bite of 23 percent. Ouch!

Exhibit 24.2 shows what happened to the stock and it gives two warnings: a bad brokerage buy signal and an earnings release.

At B, a brokerage initiated coverage with a buy recommendation just as price peaked. The smart money

Exhibit 24.5: CLX US Equity (Clorox Co/The)

Selling Head-and-Shoulders Tops

A head-and-shoulders top is one of the scarier chart patterns to see in a stock you own. Consider Exhibit 24.7, which shows a handsome one.

The squiggles on the chart become a valid head-and-shoulders top when price closes below the neckline at B.

As you look at this, one question should pop into your mind. Since the head-and-shoulders is a reversal pattern, is there something to reverse? Yes, the move up from C where the uptrend began. Price could drop that far.

What does the measure rule say? For head-and-shoulders tops, the measure rule is different than for other chart patterns. The measure rule is still based on height, but it uses the neckline instead of the full height.

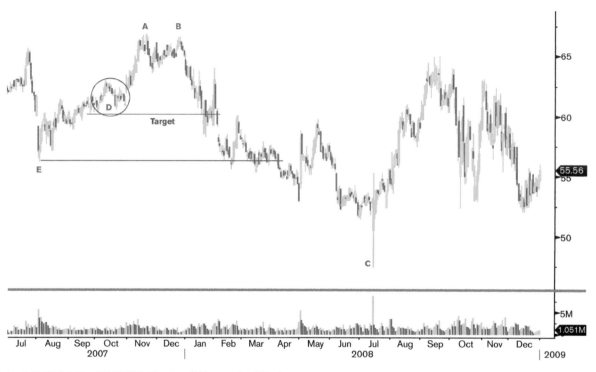

Exhibit 24.6: CLX US Equity (Clorox Co/The)

The video "Measure rule for head-and-shoulders" explains how to apply the measure rule for both head-and-shoulders top and bottoms.

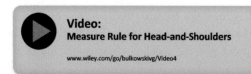

Video:
Measure Rule for Head-and-Shoulders

www.wiley.com/go/bulkowskivg/Video4

Measure the distance from the peak at the head to the neckline directly below. I show the neckline price with a small dot at A. In this example, the difference between those two is 17 − 14.47 or 2.53. Subtract the height from the breakout price, 15.05, which is the value where price crosses the neckline, to get a target of 12.52. I show the target as the top horizontal blue line.

Shoveling its way down to the target, the stock would have to dig through support formed by the flag.

Exhibit 24.7: AEIS US Equity (Advanced Energy Industries Inc)

That flag looks tight, suggesting that it could offer much to support the stock. Nothing is guaranteed, of course.

The target is also near a small knot of congestion at D. Whenever I see the target line up with support, I am reassured that the target might be real.

Below the target is more support, which I show as another blue line connecting valley C. This line has several touches or near touches extending back almost a year. Thus, if D and the target did not reverse

the decline, I would expect the stock to find support at line C. If that happened, it would mean a loss of 15.05 – 11.40 or 24 percent.

A drop to D would mean a loss of 16 percent and the target means a drop of 17 percent.

Should you sell? Exhibit 24.8 shows how the stock fared.

If you look at the price chart, the stock found support at the bottom of the flag for three months

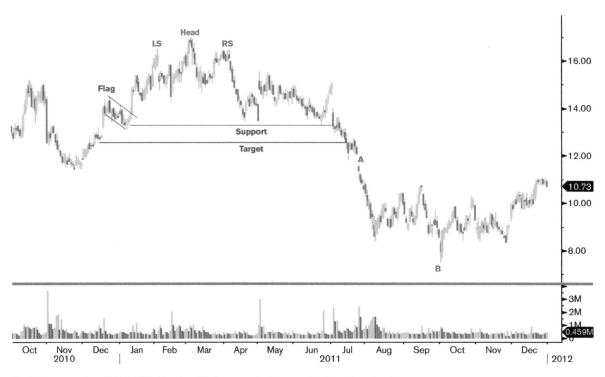

Exhibit 24.8: AEIS US Equity (Advanced Energy Industries Inc)

(the top blue line). It consolidated at the target for about a week (lower blue line) before gapping lower (A) and finally bottoming at 7.56 (B), a decline from the breakout of 50 percent.

Why did it decline so much? The entire market during this period suffered from worries about the U.S. economy and debt troubles in Europe. That giant sucking sound you may have heard was from stocks dropping during the period.

Selling Rectangles

Exhibit 24.9 shows a small rectangle top on the hard right edge. Price breaks out downward at A.

Exhibit 24.9: DTE US Equity (DTE Energy Co)

The measure rule for a rectangle is the height of the pattern subtracted from the downward breakout price. The breakout price is the value of the bottom trendline.

I do not even have to calculate it to know that the target will be above the horizontal support line I have drawn in blue. This rectangle is a wimpy one with little power to force price down. But, as we have seen in prior charts, a bear market can come along and suck the wind out of any sails, or in this case, the EPA can force costly pollution control regulations on the utilities, causing the stocks to tumble.

When looking at the big picture, the stock started moving sideways in March. Does it look tired to you, like it is ready to fall? After holding the stock for a year, you would have pocketed a gain of about 10 percent not including dividends.

Exhibit 24.10: DTE US Equity (DTE Energy Co)

If you own this stock, do you sell or hold on?

My concern is not with the rectangle because it is so small. My fear would be an extended move down that would take the stock lower, say to the mid-30s, retracing the gains back to the launch site. These flat topping patterns make me nervous.

I would wait to see what price does. If it closes below the blue support line, then I would consider selling. That would tell me the stock is ready to make a strong move down.

As Exhibit 24.10 shows, that did not happen.

The stock dropped for a few days before recovering and making a new high. The stock followed the blue trendline higher. At C, the stock made a lower high, below B. I call this pattern an ugly double top since the two peaks are not at or near the same price. When

Exhibit 24.11: ABT US Equity (Abbott Laboratories)

price confirmed a downward move at D, that was a short-term sell signal.

Selling Symmetrical Triangles

Exhibit 24.11 appears on the weekly scale, just to bind your knickers in a twist. Suppose you are a long-term holder of this stock.

The symmetrical triangle confirms with a downward breakout at A, which may be difficult to see on this chart.

A large head-and-shoulders top rests on underlying support as does the symmetrical triangle. The head-and-shoulders confirms when price closes below the neckline and it suggests a sale. I did not draw the neckline but you can guess where the intersection is at B.

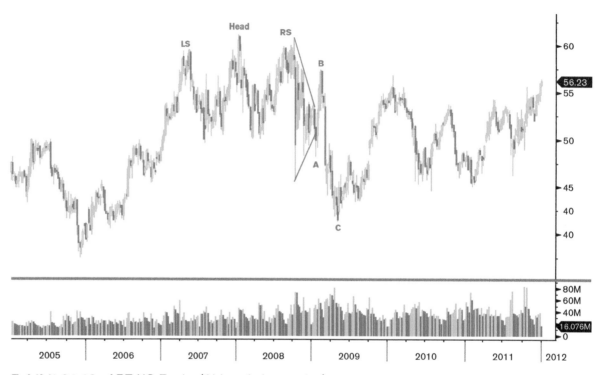

Exhibit 24.12: ABT US Equity (Abbott Laboratories)

The support line turns into overhead resistance in earlier years.

From the height of both the symmetrical triangle and the head-and-shoulders top, it is clear that a major downturn in the stock could be in the offing.

Do you sell or hold on like Bill Paxton and Helen Hunt did near the end of the movie *Twister*? Exhibit 24.12 shows what happened to the stock.

The stock broke out downward at A, as I said. Almost as quickly, the stock zipped up to B then plummeted to C. The oscillations continued over the next two years.

This is the kind of price action that swing traders love . . . if only it did not take so long. You could buy at the low of each swing and sell at the high, making money if you timed it properly.

Neither the symmetrical triangle nor the head-and-shoulders top saw price fall far enough to fulfill the measure rule. On a percentage basis, the predictions seemed too far away (about 20 to 30 percent).

Selling Triple Tops

Exhibit 24.13 shows a triple top. Pretend that you own the stock; decide whether it is time to sell. Will price continue down?

Peaks ABC form a triple top and even though the peaks are not spaced evenly, that is fine. The pattern confirms as valid when price closes below the red line, at D.

An important note is that the company announced earnings at F, the day before the breakout. We know the market did not like what it heard because the next day price closed lower, forming a closing black marubozu candlestick. Those candles act as continuation patterns, but only 52 percent of the time. That is about random, so price could reverse.

The measure rule is the height of the pattern applied to the breakout price. In this example, C is highest at 42.40 and the red line is at 38.75 for a height of 3.65. Subtracting that from the red line gives a target of 35.10, or a drop of 9.4 percent, which I show as a blue line. Price could drop much further, of course.

The three congestion areas, circled, look mean enough to stare down a price decline and support price. Between those circles and D, I do not see much in the way to catch a falling stock.

Do you sell the stock? Exhibit 24.14 shows what happened.

The triple top is at ABC and confirmation is the red line. Price plunged in a V-shaped drop, hitting the target and continuing a bit lower. Notice that the circled areas had no effect on slowing the drop at all. Or maybe they did because price halted its decline the next day.

If you held onto the stock, a week later it had recovered to the breakout price. If you survived the plunge, it means the defibrillator worked.

This chart shows what can happen after an earnings announcement, but this one is unusual. Clearly the market disliked what it heard because price tumbled in a needle-sharp plunge. But then it recovered and went on to post a new high at E. Volume increased surrounding D, but it pales in comparison to the December spike.

In this example, the measure rule worked quite well. Notice how price returned to the launch price, too, at F.

Exit Signal

The point I am making in these charts is that bearish chart patterns issue sell signals. Some predict disaster. Some do not. Signals that scare you out of a stock that then goes on to make a new high can give a false sense of security. The next time you face a similar situation, you may decide to hold on and see the stock get clobbered to the tune of a 50 percent loss.

> **KEY POINT:**
> Calculate the measure rule for triple tops by taking the height of the pattern from the highest peak to the lowest valley and subtracting it from the value of the lowest valley to get a target price. Price hits the target 48 percent of the time.

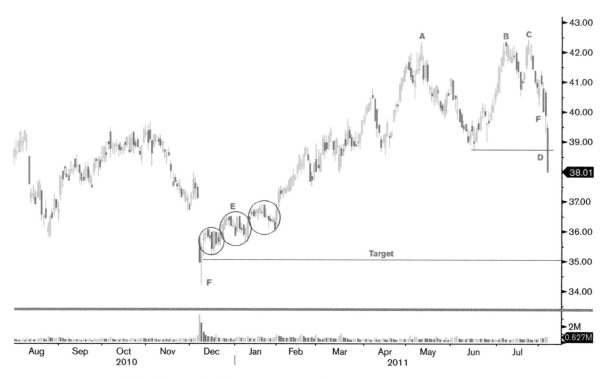

Exhibit 24.13: GAS US Equity (AGL Resources Inc)

If you obey each sell signal, you will save yourself a lot of money and your broker's smile will be as wide as the Grand Canyon. However, you will also pass up opportunities for additional gains when a stock like AGL Resources (the last exhibit) recovers in a week and eventually posts a new high.

Keep in mind that if a declining stock *does* reverse, you can always buy back in, and maybe at a lower price.

The next chapter discusses busted chart patterns. They remind me of the joke that indestructible toys are useful for breaking other toys. Yes, I loved my blocks, even if they tasted like plywood.

Exhibit 25.2: AVY US Equity (Avery Dennison Corp)

A check of the company's website reveals nothing significant between A and B.

The height of the triangle is about $1, which would bring the measure rule target close to the support line. If we assume a buy order at a penny above the top trendline, you would own the stock at about 25.85. If the stock dropped to the support line, it would mean a loss of 6 percent.

The stock at the buy price pays a dividend of 5.1 percent. Do you sell or hold on to the stock? Exhibit 25.4 shows what happened.

A 5 percent yield is a good return even for a utility stock and certainly better than the fractions of a percent that money market funds were paying at the time. That dividend can cushion a fall almost to the blue support line (see Exhibit 25.3), but you have to

Exhibit 25.3: BMY US Equity (Bristol-Myers Squibb Co)

hold the stock for a year to capture the four quarterly dividend payments.

As luck would have it, the stock bottomed on the day it broke through the lower trendline. Then it rebounded and made a nice recovery, gaining 36 percent so far. If you decided to sell and did not jump back in, you would have missed a scrumptious gain. That return does not include the dividend, too.

Busted Double Bottoms

Exhibit 25.5 shows a double bottom at AB that you may not have recognized as one. The peak between the two bottoms rises more than 10 percent above the lowest bottom and price confirms the pattern as valid when it closes above the peak at C.

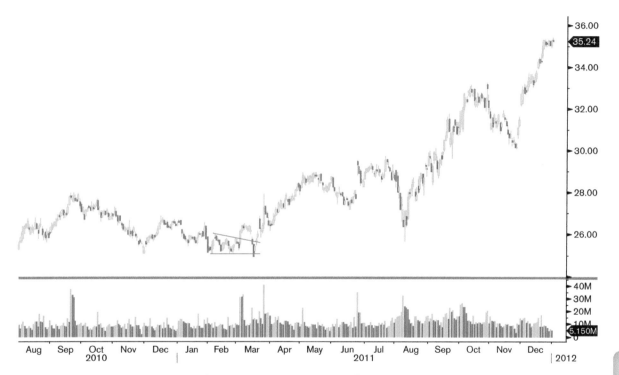

Exhibit 25.4: BMY US Equity (Bristol-Myers Squibb Co)

This double bottom appears after price drifted lower from the twin peaks at F and G. The pattern becomes a confirmed double top at D when the stock closes below H.

If the measure rule for double tops is correct, it could mean a 47 percent drop to the bottom of the gap in August 2009, at I. That is huge and hard to believe, especially in a bull market.

The stock has (breakaway) gapped lower at D, heading toward the blue support line. The stock could return to the launch price at E or drop even more. Or it could decide that busting the double bottom is all the move down it needed.

Suppose you bought the stock using a buy stop placed a penny above the breakout price. Do you sell or hold onto the stock?

DEFINITION:
Busting the double bottom

A busted double bottom occurs after price has confirmed a double bottom but climbed less than 1 percent before reversing and closing below the lowest valley in the chart pattern. The average drop of 358 busted double bottoms in a bull market was 15 percent.

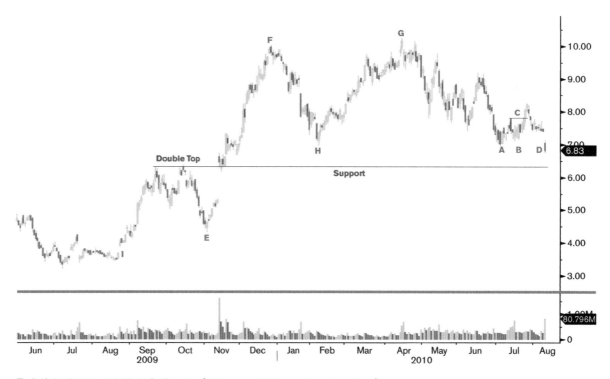

Exhibit 25.5: AMD US Equity (Advanced Micro Devices Inc)

The measure rule, which is the height of the double bottom usually added to the top of the chart pattern, can be used to predict the extent of the downward move. Subtract the height from the bottom of the chart pattern to get a target price.

Eyeballing this one, it looks as if the measure rule suggests the stock would reach the blue support line. That would mean a drop of 20 percent below the buy price. The stock is currently down 13 percent.

The smart play would have a stop already in place a penny below the lowest low. That would have limited the loss, but it would still mean a decline of 11 percent.

Exhibit 25.6 shows what happened.

I was worried that this stock would drop back to E, but the chart shows it stopped between the two

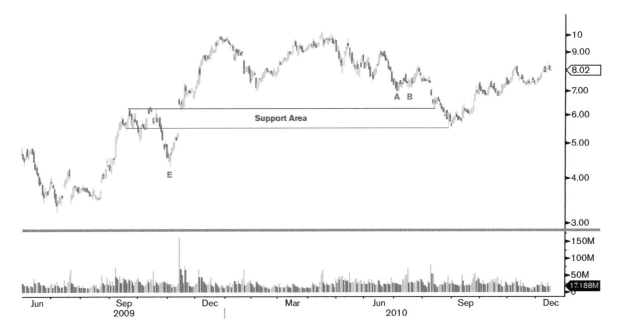

Exhibit 25.6: AMD US Equity (Advanced Micro Devices Inc)

support lines, the top one extends from a double top and the bottom one tags a few candles that bottom near the same price. It happens to line up where the stock turned in August.

The drop does not look far but on a percentage basis, it represents a decline of 29 percent. The correct answer was to have a stop in place to sell automatically when the pattern busted.

Busted Head-and-Shoulders Bottoms

The next chart shows a confirmed head-and-shoulders bottom when price closes above the neckline at A. This head-and-shoulders looks unusual because of the long neck (meaning the head is well below the shoulders). It reminds me of a pacifier that babies suck on.

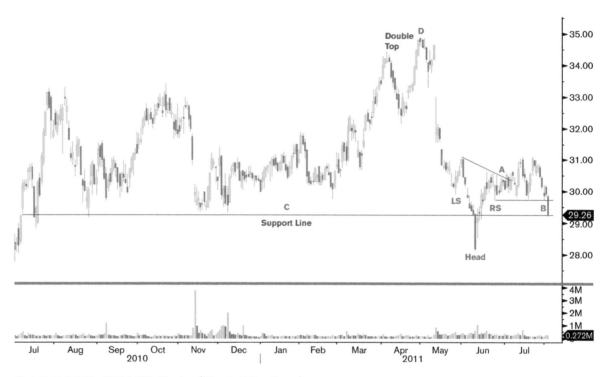

Exhibit 25.7: BKH US Equity (Black Hills Corp)

Price breaks out of a loose congestion region between A and B (the first part of which looks like a broadening top) to close near B, below the right shoulder low and at support line C. (See Exhibit 25.7.)

Notice the strong move down from peak D (part of an unusual looking double top). The head-and-shoulders reversal says that the stock is oversold and yet it appears the stock has more work to do on the downside.

My concern, given that the stock has broken out downward, is that price will attempt to form a double bottom matching the low of the head. That would mean a decline of 7 percent.

This chart shows a lot of support at line C, but not much price action below that. The longer-term chart

Exhibit 25.8: BKH US Equity (Black Hills Corp)

(not shown) shows additional support at the head low and from a descending triangle with a base at 26 in early 2010.

This is a utility stock and not some internet flyer, so the dividend would help protect a downward move. However, the head formed not because short sellers sucked too hard on the pacifier, but because the company cut earnings estimates by 20 percent.

If you own the stock, would you sell or hold on? Exhibit 25.8 shows what happened to the stock.

The stock made a V-shaped plunge to find support at the descending triangle I mentioned but not shown on the chart.

I had a hunch that the stock would form a double bottom, so I had a buy order at 28.25 that filled at A, just four cents off the day's low. That meant a yield of

5 percent, too. While the rest of the market was suffering during the fall, I made money holding this both on a capital gains basis and because of the dividend.

Busted Rectangles

Exhibit 25.9 shows a rectangle bottom that acts as a reversal pattern, but only for a few days. Price breaks out upward at A, but then busts the triangle when it closes below the bottom of it at B.

The height of this rectangle is about $1.50, so a drop to 26.90, the measure rule target, would be a loss of 10 percent below a buy price of 29.85 (a penny above the top of the rectangle).

The target is near support at the blue line, C, and near a loose congestion area circled in blue. Any of these could support price.

If the rectangle acts as a half-staff pattern, then the drop from D to the bottom of the rectangle could mirror the drop below the rectangle. That would put the target off the chart, at just below 22.

If we call that the worst case, the decline would be 27 percent. You should avoid those types of drops. In fact, why not just pick stocks that go up?

If you bought when price broke out upward from the rectangle, do you hold on or sell?

Exhibit 25.10 shows what happened.

Ouch. Price finds support near the target, C, and the loose consolidation region. This holds for several months. The company released earnings at D and the next day, E, a broker upgraded the stock. Notice how spectacularly bad the upgrade was. At F another broker upgraded the stock, and at G, the company announced earnings that no one liked. The stock started drilling toward the earth's core and bottomed at 16.09, so far, a drop of 46 percent. Selling would have been the right choice.

Busted Symmetrical Triangles

Exhibit 25.11 shows an example of what investors face when they go bottom fishing. Price started a decline from C, at 39.50, and bottomed at the symmetrical triangle, at 31.49, a drop of 20 percent. After the upward breakout from the triangle (A), was now the time to buy?

Apparently not, since a throwback (B) took price below the triangle's apex. The pattern now looked like a head-and-shoulders bottom reversal.

A support line begins from the circled area on the left and nears or touches several valleys as it extends toward the right. If price hits this, it will represent a drop of 6 percent below the buy price of 33 (a penny above the triangle trendline at the breakout).

The measure rule for the triangle, which is its height subtracted from the downward breakout price is more difficult to calculate since price broke out upward. Let us use the most recent downward trendline touch just before the breakout (32.30) in the calculation. The height is 2.32 for a target of about 30. From the buy price, the target represents a drop of 9 percent.

Do you sell or hold the stock? Exhibit 25.12 shows what the stock did.

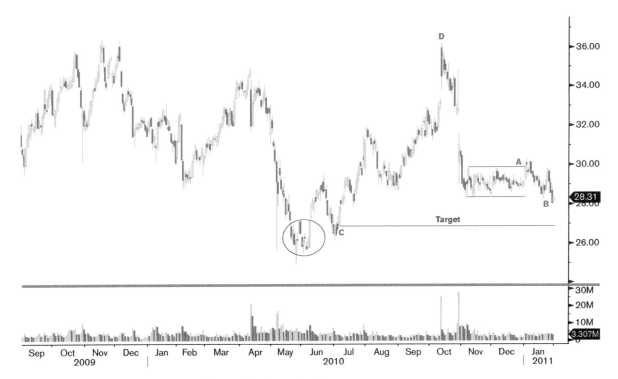

Exhibit 25.9: AVP US Equity (Avon Products Inc)

The stock dropped just 8 percent before finding support and recovering. After that, it became a moon shot.

Busted Triple Bottoms

Exhibit 25.13 shows a situation similar to the last one. Price has declined from a peak of 45.63 at F to 27.92 at E, a decline of 39 percent. The triple bottom represents a buying opportunity, so you grab the stock a penny above the highest peak, 32.41, at D.

Some joker lets air out of the tires and the stock deflates to E. A stop loss order placed below the bottom of the chart pattern would take you out automatically. However, if you forgot to place that, you would be looking at a loss of 14 percent. How far can price be expected to drop?

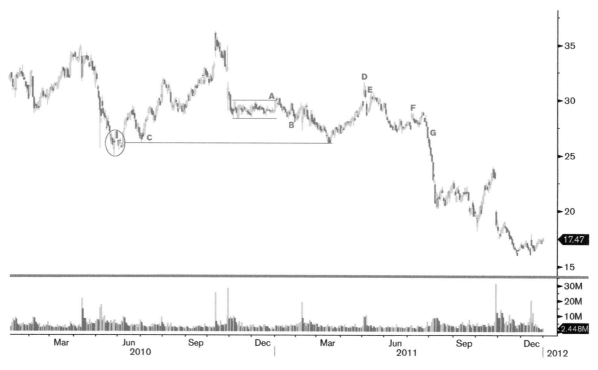

Exhibit 25.10: AVP US Equity (Avon Products Inc)

Since price is making a multi-year low, there are no recent support areas. Let us refer to the measure rule. Take the height of the triple bottom and subtract it from the bottom of the chart pattern. That gives a target of 23.78. From the buy price, that means a loss of 27 percent.

Given that you are already looking at a 14 percent hole in your wallet or purse, how much bigger do you want it to grow? Of course, the stock could reverse the next day and climb higher. After all, the stock is down 39 percent from F and even more from the April peak.

How much lower can it go? Perhaps you would like to average down, buy more shares at a lower price to drop the average cost of purchase. Do you sell, hold on, or buy more?

Exhibit 25.14 answers that.

Test Yourself

Answer the following.

1. Trade with the trend. What does that mean?
   - A. Do not short a stock in a bull market.
   - B. Do not buy a stock in a bear market.
   - C. If the market is rising, do not short a stock.
   - D. All of the above.

2. True or false: Multiply the height of a chart pattern by how often the measure rule works to get a closer price target.

3. True or false: A busted pattern sell signal means the signal did not work.

Answers: 1. C; 2. True; 3. False

CHAPTER 26

Triangle Apex Sell Signal

This chapter discusses the triangle apex sell signal, a method I have mentioned throughout this book, but one I wanted to dedicate some time to.

When any of the three varieties of triangles—ascending, descending, or symmetrical—are drawn on a chart, their apex can signal a turn in the price movement. The apex is the point where the two converging trendlines meet. Exhibit 26.1 shows examples.

Look at descending triangle A in the middle of the chart. Directly above the apex, I have drawn a blue line to A. Notice that the line meets the peak—a short-term turning point.

Descending triangle B, to the left, is not as successful as A in forecasting the turn. Above its apex is B. The small minor low is a few days away from the blue line. In this example, price did not turn at the apex, but it was close.

Ascending triangle C also appears to work well, but it is hard to tell in the congested area. The apex occurs within a day of minor low C.

Testing

I used 500 stocks from July 1991 to July 1996 on the three triangle types and found all minor highs and lows during that period. Then I compared them to where the triangle apex appeared.

I found that the average distance from the apex to a minor high or low was 3.6 days.

A benchmark used a month's worth of data on each side of the apex and measured the average distance between peaks or valleys. It was 13.1 days. If the apex were located between those peaks or valleys, it would be half the distance, or 6.55 days.

This is like standing between two trees 13 feet apart. If you stand in the middle, each one of them would be 6.5 feet away.

The apex has to be closer than the average, and it is: 3.6 days versus the average's 6.55 days. Using the apex as a turning point works better than chance suggests.

In two other tests, I visually compared the triangle's apex to a minor high or low (within a few days)

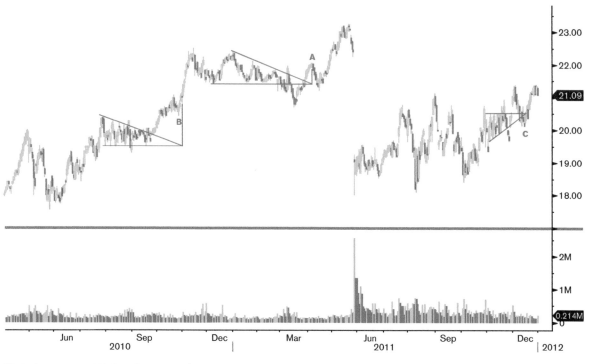

Exhibit 26.1: EDE US Equity (Empire District Electric Co/The)

and counted how often the method worked. One test succeeded 75 percent of the time (165 out of 221 triangles).

Another test using computer drawn triangles (which are less accurate) showed matches 60 percent of the time (144 out of 239). Both used data from October 2006 to January 2008. In other words, this method works at least 60 percent of the time.

Trading

Look at Exhibit 26.2 for a trading example.

Symmetrical triangle A forms between two converging trendlines that meet at apex C. Directly above the apex is B, a major turning point.

Regardless of the time scale, which could be the 1-minute scale, or monthly (this one is daily), the

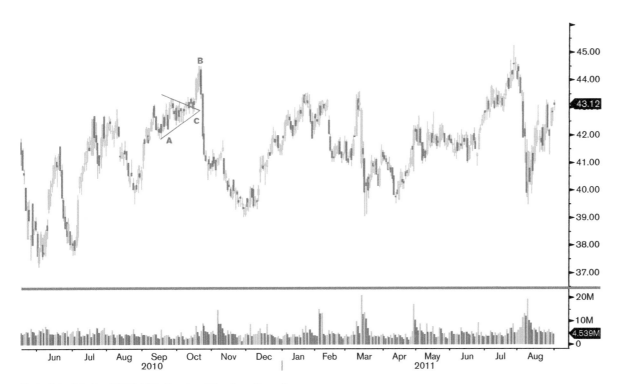

Exhibit 26.2: EXC US Equity (Exelon Corp)

alignment of the apex with price is a good time to take profits in this example.

Few triangles will show such dramatic turns. Remember that the turn is within four days of the apex, on average. If you are a short-term trader, like a swing or day trader, this visual technique can help you decide when to sell.

Page through this book and compare the many triangles shown with their apex turning points to see how often this technique works, how well it works, and how big the turns tend to be.

When trading a triangle, look for prior examples of triangles in the same stock to see how well the technique works.

SMART INVESTOR TIP

Find triangles in the historical price series to see how this apex method worked in the past. That will help you gauge how well it could work in the future.

Test Yourself

Answer the following.

1. What is meant by the apex of a triangle?
   A. It is where the triangle begins.
   B. It is where the triangle ends.
   C. It is where the trendlines join.

2. True or false: The date of a triangle's apex works most of the time as a future price turning point.

3. True or false: Ascending and descending triangles have one and only one horizontal trendline, but symmetrical triangles have no horizontal trendlines.

Answers: 1. C; 2. True; 3. True

CHAPTER 27

Trendline Sell Signals

Trendlines are wonderful trading tools and sometimes they even work! This chapter examines up-sloping trendlines as sell signals to see how well they behave and how to use them.

I have used trendlines to outline pattern boundaries throughout this book. This chapter looks at trendlines not as pattern markers, but as selling tools. Those tools alert us to trend changes and issue exit signals. Our task is to judge how important those signals are.

Chapter 3 discussed how to draw trendlines, chart scales (log or linear), the three types of trendlines (internal, external, and curved), and guidelines for using them. Refer to Chapter 3 if you need a review.

Exhibit 27.1 shows how effective a trendline sell signal can be.

This chart is on the daily scale, and it is a scary one. Imagine buying the stock at B, seeing it climb to D, and then tumbling to the August low, below the purchase price. How many of us have invested in such stocks? I

have. Preventing such situations is where trendlines can help.

I started drawing the trendline at B and it slices through A because both points seemed to create a trendline that hugs price better.

At C, the company announced earnings. The market's reaction to the news was a yawn. Price spiked down that day and during the next week, it rounded over, but recovered quickly enough.

At D, the company settled litigation that cost the company $39 million over claims related to an acquisition in 2004. The announcement pushed the stock down, and it could have been the catalyst that started the downtrend.

Price closed below the trendline, which was a sell signal, and at E, the company complained of weak demand from the government. That began a waterfall drop that splashed down at 21.86 in mid-August, a drop of 32 percent from the close at E.

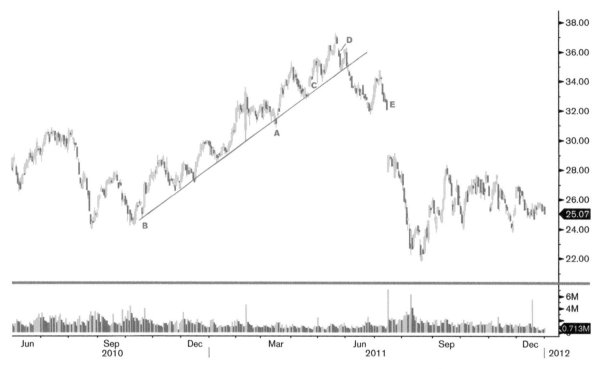

Exhibit 27.1: FLIR US Equity (FLIR Systems Inc)

Even if you were late taking the trendline sell signal, you could have saved a lot of money by selling.

Trendline Selling

Exhibit 27.2 shows various trendlines used as sell signals.

This chart is on the weekly scale. You may find it helpful to switch to a longer period when trading trendlines. That will force you to ignore market noise and concentrate on the longer-term trend. For example, if you day trade, use the daily chart. If you use end-of-day data on the daily chart, switch to the weekly and so on.

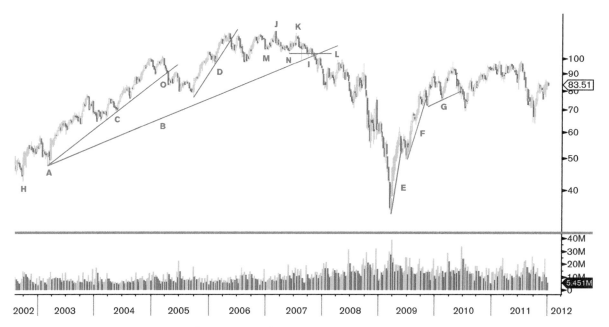

Exhibit 27.2: FDX US Equity (FedEx Corp)

Trendline B begins at A instead of at H because it seemed to fit price better. The line pierces price at I and that is the sell signal.

Notice peak K is lower than J and it confirms when price closes below horizontal line L. Valley N is below minor low M. Price making lower highs and lower lows is another clue to a trend change from up to down.

When price closed below I, it was the signal that told the smart money to sell.

Look at trendline C. It also issued a sell signal at O when price closed below it. This time, however, the drop did not last long. Another trendline, D, formed. This one had a steeper slope and that was unusual. A close below the line was also a sell signal.

Notice trendlines E, F, and G. See how a very steep trendline (E) gives way to a new trend that is not as steep (F) and even trendline F yields to G. Trendlines with a 45-degree slope or less tend to have staying power. Steeper than that and they tend to flame out quickly.

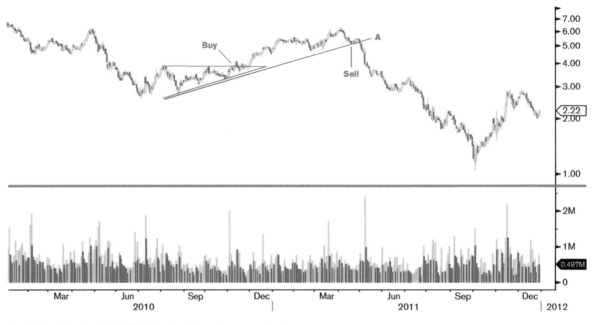

Exhibit 27.3: HW US Equity (Headwaters Inc)

Get into the practice of drawing trendlines beneath price in a rising trend. If price closes below the line, it is an indication that the trend has weakened. Perhaps, just perhaps, it is time to sell.

Triangle Sale

Exhibit 27.3 shows blue line A parallel to the ascending bottom trendline (the line should be on top of the triangle, but I drew it parallel for clarity). When price *closes* below this line, it represents a sell signal.

Use a stop loss order for the first month or two and *if price trends,* then wait for a close below the trendline as a potential sell signal.

In this example, the buy price is at 3.90 and the sell signal is at 5.31 (the opening price the day after price closes below the trendline. Remember, the blue line is drawn slightly below where it should be

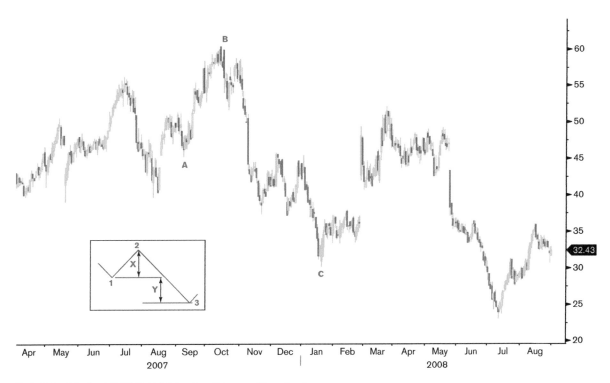

Exhibit 28.2: HURC US Equity (Hurco Cos Inc)

Test Yourself

Answer true or false to the following statements:

1. The swing rule works only for small swings.
2. The swing rule is the same as the measure rule except that it applies to trendlines.
3. Use the swing rule to predict price turning points.

Answers: 1.False; 2. False; 3. True

CHAPTER 29

A Tale of Two Trades

In this book, we started with the basics: trendlines, gaps, throwbacks, support and resistance, and a few other flavors to spice up the text. Following that was pattern identification of chart patterns formed by horizontal lines, diagonal ones, and then bumps such as double tops and head-and-shoulders.

I discussed visual buy and sell signals, and that is where chart patterns excel. With each breakout, a trader is given the opportunity to make money in a stock or exit a position before it takes an ambulance ride.

Trading chart patterns is easy, but making money using them is not. Chart patterns work only when the market trends. If the stock moves sideways, the industry decides to speed into a brick wall, or the general market drops into a sinkhole, your chances of making money using any technique diminish.

Take what you have learned within the covers of this book, shape it to fit your needs and trading style, and then apply it to the markets. Learn from your mistakes and your successes. Track your progress and over time, you may find that your balance sheet changes from bleeding red to throwing off green in the color of money.

Before you finish this book, let me share a new trading setup.

Trade Entry

Exhibit 29.1 shows two trades I made beginning with broadening bottom A. We have not covered broadening bottoms, but they have nothing to do with weight loss. Rather, the pattern sports two diverging trendlines. The top one slopes upward following a series of peaks and the bottom one hugs valleys.

Two days after price bounced off the lower trendline, I turned into a vulture and pounced, buying the stock at A. I wrote in my notebook, "The stock is cheap and shows support at this level. Oil prices are high, meaning fuel costs will continue to hurt, interest rates are rising and expected to move up ¼ point next Wednesday at the FOMC (Federal Reserve) meeting."

FAST FACTS

Broadening bottoms break out upward 53 percent of the time.

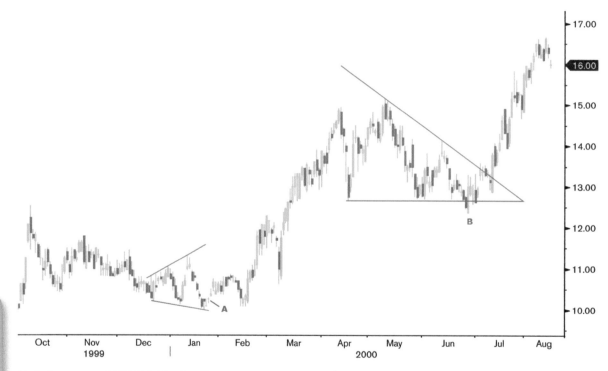

Exhibit 29.1: LUV US Equity (Southwest Airlines Co)

I felt the stock was at a good price to add to an exist-ing position. However, I was worried that the stock could tumble through the bottom of the chart pattern, given that the general market was trendline lower at the time.

The winds were favorable and the airline's stock took to the skies and soared like a hawk riding a Texas thermal. Then the winds blew in another chart pat-tern in the shape of a descending triangle.

Trade Exit

The descending triangle is a pattern we discussed. The beast breaks out downward most often, so it worried me. The size of the chart pattern suggested a decline of at least 15 percent (the measure rule).

Here is what I wrote about the sale. "I sold my posi-tion because the stock has pierced the support base of a descending triangle. With seasonal performance moving up in December and peaking in the spring, I missed the high by about $3 per share. Ouch. Oil prices are high, leading to rising fuel costs, and interest rates are still high, maybe moving up more. So, it looks like the excitement is over although today the stock is up almost $1."

I made 27 percent on the trade, including a small dividend payment.

As the chart shows, the stock flew to new highs, but I watched from the airport. However, it could just as easily have dropped back to my buy price at A, or lower. My trading plan said that if the stock closed below the bottom of the chart pattern, sell. I did.

The Setup

On its surface, the two trades are nothing remarkable. I bought at a bullish chart pattern and sold after the breakout from a bearish one.

How would a trading setup based on that idea perform? Load the champagne bucket with ice, chill your favorite brew, and then I will tell you a bedtime story about how I tested the setup.

I have a database of 500 stocks that spans from mid-1991 to mid-1996 which I use to test stock market theories. I have pored over the database multiple times looking for and cataloging chart patterns. The computer simulation I ran used that database on the chart patterns discussed in this book.

Here are the three rules:

1. Buy when the stock breaks out upward from a chart pattern.
2. After entry, place a stop loss order a penny below the bottom of the chart pattern.
3. Hold until price breaks out downward from another chart pattern or price hits the stop.

I tested 17 types of chart patterns but removed ascending and symmetrical triangles when *buying* because they suck as entry signals. However, they were used to exit the stock.

The chart patterns tested were:

- Ascending and symmetrical triangles for exit signals only
- Descending triangles
- Four types of Adam and Eve combinations of double tops and bottoms (eight patterns total)
- Head-and-shoulders tops and bottoms
- Rectangle tops and bottoms
- Triple tops and bottoms

I did not trail the stop upward. I just let the stock move between two chart patterns.

Results

The following table shows the results for bull markets. The in-sample column covers July 1991 to July 1996. The out-of-sample and 200 SMA columns cover the period from 1996 through January 2012 using a larger database but one less scoured. Open trades use the most recent close available. Commissions were $10 per trade ($20 round trip).

The results between the in and out-of-sample periods were comparable in many areas. The win/loss ratio dropped from 59 to 48 percent, but that could be due to more than three times as many out-of-sample trades. The hold time probably changed for the same reason.

The maximum loss of 72 percent relates to a trade in Coldwater Creek using a tall double bottom at a low price. The stock price nearly tripled from the buy price in 2009, but ran into trouble in recent years, giving back its gains and more. I did not log any bearish chart patterns after the buy, so price stopped out the trade when it slid below the bottom of the chart pattern.

The table's far right column shows an additional buy rule, that of entering a trade only if the breakout price is *below* the 200-day simple moving average (SMA). I used the same out-of-sample data as described earlier.

Patterns with breakouts *above* the 200-day SMA performed worse. That may come as a shock to many of you, but I have seen it before. Some traders just assume that waiting for price to rise above the 200-day SMA will help performance. Test it both ways to be sure.

Closing Position

This setup shows that buying and selling chart patterns can be profitable over the intermediate and long term for investors and position traders.

Swing traders can benefit from trading tall rectangles as price ping-pongs between the two trendlines. Day traders can use chart patterns as entry signals and exit at the measure rule target.

Should you profit from the advice in this book, tell your friends and neighbors, post a customer review at Amazon.com, and then put me in your will.

Trade well.

	In-Sample	Out-of-Sample	< 200 SMA
Number of trades	1,333	4,185	1,685
Win/loss	59%	48%	50%
Average profit/loss	27%	25%	26%
Average hold time (days)	325 days	254 days	247 days
Maximum loss	−40%	−72%	−72%
Average win	52%	62%	63%
Average loss	−11%	−11%	−11%

Test Yourself

Answer true or false to the following statements:

1. Broadening bottoms follow two converging trend-lines.

2. A downward breakout from a descending triangle means price is going to drop substantially.

3. Exhibit 29.1 shows a busted descending triangle.

Answers: 1. False; 2. False; 3. True

Bloomberg Functionality Cheat Sheet

Currencies

FXIP	FX information portal
FXTF	FX ticker finder
FXC	Currency rates matrix
WCR	World currency rates
WCRS	World currency ranker

Money Markets

PGM	Program lookup
MMR	Money rate monitors
BBAL	BBA Libor fixings
CPHS	Direct issuer CP rates
MMCV	Money-market curves

Government Bonds

BTMM	Treasury and money-market monitor
SOVM	Sovereign debt monitor
WB	World bond markets
GGR	Generic government rates
CRVF	Curve finder

Corporate Bonds

SECF	Security finder
NIM	New issue monitor for bonds
TRAC	TRACE home page
FICM	Fixed income credit monitor
YCRV	Yield curve analysis

Stocks

ECDR	Equity offerings
WEI	World equity indexes
MOST	Most active stocks
MOV	Index movers*
EQS	Equity screening

Commodities

SECF	Security finder
GLCO	Global commodity prices and data
NRG	Bloomberg Energy Service menu
MINE	Metals, minerals, and mining menu
AGRS	Agricultural markets menu

Real Estate

RE	Real estate menu
CRE	Commercial real estate data
RMEN	Global indexes
REUS	U.S. real estate
HSST	U.S. housing data

Futures

SECF	Security finder
CTM	Contract table menu
WEIF	World equity index futures
WBF	World bond futures
FRD	Currency spot and forward rates

Options

MOSO	Most active options
OMON	Option monitor*
CALL	Call option monitor*
PUT	Put option monitor*
OMST	Most active contracts*

Swaps

IRSB	Interest rate swap rates
WS	World swap matrix
USSW	U.S. swap market
CDS	Credit default swap overview
GCDS	Global CDS monitor

Funds

FUND	Funds and portfolio holdings
MHD	Mutual fund holdings*
EXTF	Exchange-traded products
HFND	Hedge fund home page
PE	Private equity home page

*Security-specific function

Pipe Tops

Rectangle Bottoms

Rectangle Tops

Rounding Bottoms

Rounding Tops

Scallops, Ascending

Scallops, Ascending and Inverted

Scallops, Descending

Scallops, Descending and Inverted

Three Falling Peaks

Three Rising Valleys

Triangles, Ascending

Triangles, Descending

Triangles, Symmetrical

Triple Bottoms

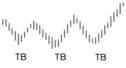

TB   TB   TB

Triple Tops

TT   TT   TT

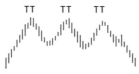

Wedges, Falling

Wedges, Rising

Bibliography

Brown, T. Sullivan, and Sperandeo, Victor. *Trader Vic –
Methods of a Wall Street Master.* New York: John
Wiley & Sons, 1991, 1993.

Bulkowski, Thomas N. *Encyclopedia of Chart Patterns,
Second Edition.* Hoboken, NJ: John Wiley & Sons,
2005.

Bulkowski, Thomas N. *Encyclopedia of Candlestick
Charts.* Hoboken, NJ: John Wiley & Sons, 2008.

Bulkowski, Thomas N. *Getting Started in Chart Patterns.* Hoboken, NJ: John Wiley & Sons, 2006.

Bulkowski, Thomas N. *Trading Classic Chart Patterns.*
New York: John Wiley & Sons, 2002.

Weinstein, Stan. *Secrets for Profiting in Bull and Bear
Markets.* New York: McGraw-Hill, 1988.

About the Author

Thomas N. Bulkowski is a successful investor with 30 years of experience trading stocks. He is considered to be a leading expert on chart patterns and is also an internationally known author of the John Wiley & Sons titles: *Encyclopedia of Chart Patterns, Second Edition; Getting Started in Chart Patterns; Encyclopedia of Candlestick Charts;* and *Trading Classic Chart Patterns.*

Bulkowski is a frequent contributor to *Active Trader* and *Technical Analysis of Stocks & Commodities* magazines. Before earning enough from his investments to "retire" from his day job at age 36, he was a hardware design engineer at Raytheon and a senior software engineer for Tandy Corporation.

His website address is www.thepatternsite.com. There you will have free access to hundreds of articles, research, and blog posts written by Bulkowski.

Other books by Thomas Bulkowski:

- *Encyclopedia of Candlestick Charts*
- *Encyclopedia of Chart Patterns*
- *Evolution of a Trader: Fundamental Analysis and Position Trading*
- *Evolution of a Trader: Swing and Day Trading*
- *Evolution of a Trader: Trading Basics*
- *Getting Started in Chart Patterns*
- *Trading Classic Chart Patterns*

Index

321